# A CHILD'S HEART
# AND A CHILD'S DREAMS

## SRI CHINMOY

# A CHILD'S HEART
# AND A CHILD'S DREAMS

## SRI CHINMOY

ISBN: 0-88497-862-1
Library of Congress card catalog no.: 86-082090

Published by:
Aum Publications
86-24 Parsons Blvd.
Jamaica, NY 11432

# INTRODUCTION

Many years ago I asked Sri Chinmoy the question, "Is there a particular spiritual quality to invoke while teaching our children?" His answer was brief and is included in this book. The key word in that answer is "self-giving." Honestly speaking, at the time I wasn't sure just what that word meant. In time, however, it became for me not only a goal to work towards but more and more a way of life. Sri Chinmoy says:

> A mother gives and gives to her child simply because she loves him. If she is lucky enough, when the child grows up he will give to her in return. But very often he does not return her offering. He has his own life. But as the mother gives, she is blessed by God. The light, affection and other divine qualities which she gives to her child are blessings in themselves.

Through the profound communication with God that we call meditation, we can tap the wellspring of peace, love and light that resides deep within. To bring forward these qualities is to transform our own lives and the lives of our children and to discover real fulfilment. We can then offer these qualities not only to our families and friends, but to all of humanity.

Inner and outer transformation can only take place if parents make a conscious effort to nurture themselves and their children with spiritual sustenance. Modern society has placed our children in one of the most precarious positions of any group of youngsters in history. In their everyday lives they are faced with temptations which may have never before lured such youthful targets. In a larger sense, many have a very real concern for the survival of our planet. It has never been more imperative for parents to offer their children constant love and concern which, in fact, is none other than God's Love. Further, a child can be taught to find this love himself, in his own heart. He then becomes a beautiful flower of self-giving. As Sri Chinmoy says, "If you can inspire your child with love, then he will inspire someone else with love. It is from one that we come to many."

In this book Sri Chinmoy offers practical advice on a subject that is not only an idealist's dream, but a concerned parent's lifeline: fostering your child's spiritual life, so that he grows up with love for God and a heart of self-giving to all. For thirteen years my family has lived under the loving guidance of Sri Chinmoy. I have witnessed the inner blossoming not only of our daughter but also of the children of Sri Chinmoy's other disciples, sustained by the philosophy contained in this book.

It is not necessarily easy to teach a child to meditate or to give him or her constant loving concern in the face of a parent's mundane routines. It can be a challenge to offer discipline and strength as well as love. Sri Chinmoy and his illumining philosophy have made this more possible than I could ever have imagined. The children I know who have been touched by Sri Chinmoy's wisdom have come to embody the loving hearts and peaceful lives inherent in true spirituality. In their lives the quality of self-giving is understood. For this, we, their parents, will forever remain profoundly grateful.

*Atar*

# CONTENTS

# PART ONE

# A GUIDE FOR PARENTS

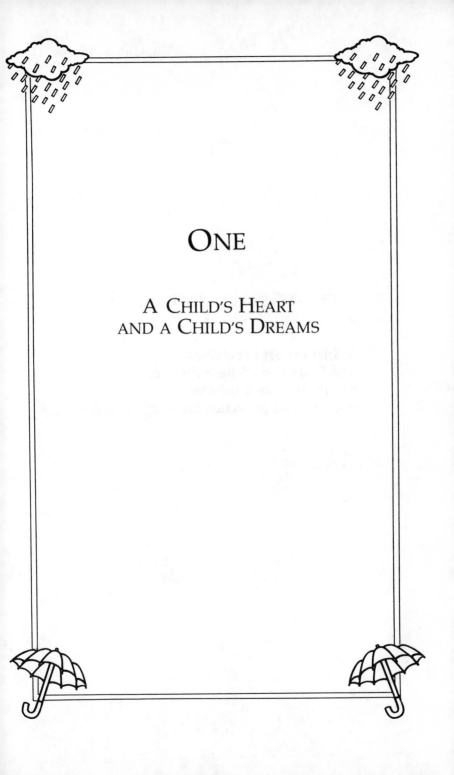

# ONE

## A CHILD'S HEART
## AND A CHILD'S DREAMS

## A CHILD'S SWEET HOPEFULNESS

A child's sweet hopefulness
And God's immediate fruitfulness
Are always found together
In a beautiful perfection-satisfaction-garden.

# 1

GOD'S creation is like a lotus or a rose. Each petal is unique in its own way. A child is an especially significant part of God's creation, since God is dreaming in and through every child and manifesting Himself in an unprecedented way. Each child is bringing down a new message from God which was not known before. Naturally, if the world accepts it, the world is getting new light, new power, new joy and new love.

On today's child depends tomorrow's future. We talk about perfection, but this perfection that we speak of will come only from children—from a child's heart and a child's dreams. The old creation has to surrender to the new. The old creation means the life that does not want to see the truth, accept the truth or fulfil the truth. Who wants to see, accept and fulfil the truth? The child. Only a child has the capacity to feel that every day is a new dawn. Only a child is inspired to run, to do something, to give something to the world every day.

## *The significance of a child*

It is a child, not an old person, who makes
progress in life. Old people do not care for
progress. But mere years do not make a person
old. Somebody who is sixty or seventy years of
age may have the enthusiasm, inner joy and
inspiration of a child. Again, there will be
people seventeen, eighteen or nineteen years
old who have no aspiration, no inspiration, no
dynamism. If a boy of nineteen does not have
the capacity to draw something from the world
or to offer something to the world, if he does
not care for the world and feels that he does
not need anything from the world, then he is
ninety-nine years old in spirit. On the other
hand, if somebody of ninety-nine wants to
learn the inner language—the language of
divine love, the language of divine peace, the
language of divine wisdom, the language of
divine light—then he is a child in spirit. In the
spiritual life we are not concerned with earthly
years but with an individual's inner eagerness
to do something and to become something—to
become a child of God.

If you really want to become a child, then
you have to feel that there is always something
to learn and that God is there to teach you. In
the spiritual life you are learning something
every day, every hour, every minute, every
second from our divine Father. If you constantly have the feeling that you are learning in the
inner world, there is no end to the God-divinity
that you can receive and achieve.

## A childlike heart

Because a child lives in the heart, he always feels that his mother or his father will take care of him. All the time he feels that there is protection, there is guidance, there is assistance. So naturally he has confidence in his life. Because he is always in the heart, he feels that there is no need which his parents will not fulfil. If he lived in the mind, he would immediately think, "Oh, perhaps my father will not be able to do this. Perhaps my mother will not be there to help me." Then he would become fearful, doubtful and anxious. But a child does not live in the mind. Similarly, if you want to have a childlike spirit, no matter how old you are, you have to feel that there is Someone with infinitely more Wisdom-Light who is constantly thinking of you, guiding you and protecting you, and that this Person is God.

He who cares more for the intellect than for the heart, he who cares more for the outer achievement than for the inner achievement, he who cares more for society around him than for God within him, can never act like a child. A true child lives all the time in the heart, whereas a grown-up is all the time in the mind. In the mind there is no love. Real love can be found only inside the flower-heart. The flower-heart tries all the time to make others happy. Because God has the flower-heart of a child, He is trying all the time to make us happy. A child's flower-heart is a divine heart. If we remain in the outer world, we see children as ordinary human beings. But if we go within, then we immediately see that children embody all the divine qualities of God. At that time we see children as true miracles—as divine instruments, as flowers of God.

It is especially the parents who have to see their children in this way. If the parents feel that their children are flowers of God, then the parents will make the children not only feel this but also grow into this. It is the parents who, right from the beginning, have to see the divinity in their children and make their children see the divinity within themselves. That is the parents' supreme role. It is not enough for the parents to feed and clothe their children and send them to school. No, the parents must take responsibility for bringing out their children's divine qualities.

All children can and must be reached spiritually. It is infinitely easier to reach children spiritually than to reach them any other way. For children are nothing but fresh and beautiful flowers ready to be placed on the altar of God the Truth, God the Light and God the Delight.


*Question:* Do children see more beauty than grown-ups do?

*Sri Chinmoy:* Yes, children always see more beauty than grown-ups do, because children remain more in the heart and the soul. Because of their tremendous inner purity, even in darkness they see beauty and light. When the mind is developed, this undivine mind immediately tries to see impurity even in light, even in wisdom, even in something progressive. The human mind gets satisfaction by seeing ugliness. But a child does not use the mind. He takes everything as his very own, so he sees beauty in everyone and in everything. He feels that there is nothing which is absolutely undivine, which is perfectly true.

*Question:* How can we fulfil the hearts and souls of the children of the world?

*Sri Chinmoy:* We can fulfil the hearts and souls of the children of the world only by becoming the hearts and souls of the children of the world. What does that mean? At every moment we must cultivate an eagerness to learn things that are illumining and fulfilling. At every moment we must have the enthusiasm and eagerness to learn more about truth, more about light, more about delight. It is our eagerness to learn that will give us a childlike heart and a childlike soul. And it is only by having a childlike heart and a childlike soul that we can fulfil the hearts and souls of the children of the world.

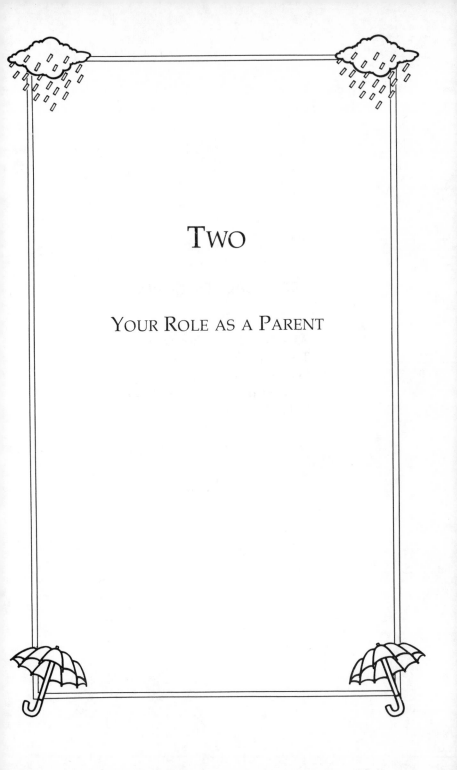

# TWO

## YOUR ROLE AS A PARENT

## GOD   REACHES   DOWN

As a mother reaches down
To offer a fruit to her child,
Even so God the Infinite
Reaches down to offer Himself
   To the finite.

# 2

T HE sacred and divine purpose of the family is to help each individual member to discover his own real reality. If an individual does not discover the real reality in himself, then he is denying the promise that he made to God. What is this promise? Once upon a time when he was in the soul's region, he promised to realise, to reveal and to manifest God on earth. In order to fulfil that promise he chose to take birth in one particular family rather than in any of the millions of other families on earth. It is in this family that the child's physical and spiritual development take place during his formative years.

When you are blessed with a child, you bring into your life a solid portion of divinity from above. At that time, your soul makes another solemn promise to God: that you will make your child a perfect instrument of God. Either you will be in a position to help your child yourself or you will take the help of some other human being. This is your soul's promise.

American parents often confuse lack of discipline with love and concern. When it is a matter of deep love and concern, they do not give it. And when it is a matter of strict spiritual discipline, inner discipline, they are certainly not giving it to their children. Their children are not properly moulded with inner or outer discipline. They are not properly taught either on the spiritual plane or on the physical and mental planes.

### Freedom and discipline

Here in the West, there is a kind of freedom that I do not endorse. Parents sometimes act out of false modesty, saying that they do not know what is best for their children. So they give their children the freedom to find out for themselves what is best. True, in comparison to a spiritual Master or a Yogi you may know nothing. But in comparison to your children, you know much more. You have made many mistakes in life, and by making mistakes you have come to know to some extent what is good and what is bad. If you really love your children, you will let them profit from your experience. Every day you should pray to God and meditate on God to illumine you so you will not misguide your children. And the illumination you get, you have to offer to your children. So in the children's formative years, the parents should always tell their children what is best for them.

If children are not properly moulded when they are of a tender age, then when they grow up they may take drugs and do many undivine things. At that time the parents claim, "I didn't teach them to do these things." But unfortunately the parents gave them the wrong kind of freedom. Instead of teaching their own ideals to their children, they let the children make up their own minds.

When you have a child, you give your child milk because you know that it is nutritious. You do not say, "Let the child drink milk or water, whichever he prefers, and when he gets older he will realise that milk is better for him." By that time he may have fallen sick or even died. So you make the child drink milk until he is ten or twelve years old and then, if he does not like milk, you let him drink something else.

Likewise, on the spiritual plane, parents often do not feed their children's souls. They say that they do not know which path their children will want, which church they need or what kind of prayer is best for them, so they do not teach them anything. But what you feel is best for your own inner lives, you should also feel is good for your children. Children will die spiritually if you don't give them inner nourishment. You are not injecting anything into them; you are giving them food. They may not like that particular food, but they have to eat or they will die. Later, when they grow up, they will have the freedom to eat whatever they choose.

Here I see thousands of children who have been misguided by their parents in the name of freedom. Freedom is available, but who can really enjoy freedom? He who listens to the dictates of his inner being and obeys the inner law. You enjoy freedom on the outer plane precisely because you listen to a higher authority, which is your own higher self. When you do not listen to your higher self, at that time you are totally limited and bound.

The parents have to feel that since they have
more wisdom and experience than their
children, they are the higher self of their
children. They are part and parcel of their
existence, but they are more conscious;
therefore, they are in a position to guide their
children. These same children will one day
grow up and be in a position to guide and
mould their own children. But when children
are given freedom before they have any inner
wisdom, this freedom is not good.

*Material wealth and love*

In America, parents always think that they
have to give their children material things. But
when it is a matter of love, most American
parents do not give it to their children. They
give a life of comfort. But there is a great
difference between a life of comfort and a life
of love. The child's heart and soul do not care
for money. In the depths of his own heart the
child cares only for the mother's heart, the
father's heart. If the child gets love from his
parents, then he is eternally and divinely bound
by his parents and he himself binds his parents
in the same way.

Love has to be given unconditionally, not
with the feeling of an inner bargain. If the parents think that they will love their child when
he is four so that when he is twenty-five he will
give them material comfort, this is absurd. God
is constantly showering His choicest Blessings
on us. He never cares for our gratitude. He
cares only for His giving. When He is giving,
He is happy. In this world, happiness comes

only from giving. So the mother and father should give everything to their children unconditionally and expect nothing in return for their love. True, if the parents go on pouring their love into their children, eventually their children *will* offer them gratitude. But real parents do not care for gratitude; they care only for loving their children. Even if the children do not offer gratitude, at least one person will never remain ungrateful for what the parents have given to them, and that person is God. He will try to please the parents in His own divine way.

## The mother's love

The dictionary houses thousands and millions of words, but without the least possible hesitation I wish to say that the word 'mother' remains unparalleled in terms of sweetness, love, concern, intimacy, closeness and oneness. There is no other word as significant as 'mother'. The mother is affection, the mother is love, the mother is concern, the mother is closeness, the mother is inseparable oneness with the child. In the life of the mother, the child is undoubtedly the dearest living being. And in the heart of the child, the same experience must always loom large—the mother is all. To the child, the mother is sweet, sweeter, sweetest. To the mother, the child is sweeter than the sweetest.

A mother gives and gives to her child simply because she loves him. If she is lucky enough, when the child grows up he will give to her in return. But very often he does not return her offering. He has his own life. But as the mother gives, she is blessed by God. The light, affection and other divine qualities which she gives to her child are blessings in themselves.

In a mother's love we see divinity expressing itself in various significant ways. The first thing we notice in a mother's love is purest concern, and the second thing we notice is endless patience. In a father's love we will not find that kind of infinite patience; we will find wisdom and other things. But in a mother's love, in addition to wisdom we will find infinite patience. The mother is ready to wait for the child to grow up and learn everything. The father is to some extent impatient. The father judges the child according to his own light, peace, wisdom and knowledge, whereas the mother judges the child according to the child's capacity.

The love that a child gets from his mother is more fruitful than the love that he gets from his father. When it is a matter of inner intimacy, it is the mother's love that is more successful. When we feel something vast, immediately it is our father-love that comes to the fore. But when we feel the intensity of two hearts, we immediately think of the love between mother and child.

The child knows that the mother will not do anything intentionally to harm him. The child believes that even unconsciously she will not do anything wrong. The child has such implicit faith in the mother. He feels that if someone had poison, the mother herself would drink the poison to save him. This kind of faith we will see in the child only before his mind develops. Once the mind starts functioning at the age of thirteen or so, at that time the sweet intimacy between mother and child is broken, for the mind has its own way of doubting and suspecting.

## Seeing God in your child

As parents, you should feel that your children are dear to you precisely because God is inside them. Again, you should feel that you are dear to your children because God is inside you. While you are talking to your children and trying to discipline their lives, you have to feel the presence of the living God inside them. The way to feel the presence of God inside your children is to feel His presence inside yourself first. Then it is easy to see the presence of God inside others. If you maintain your own divinity within yourself, then no matter whom you see, that person will be a projection of your own divinity.

Unfortunately, most people do not feel the presence of God inside themselves, let alone inside their children. They look upon their children as their possessions and feel that they have every right to mould them and guide them according to their own sweet will. But if you can feel that you love your children precisely because God is inside them, then there will be a spontaneous flow of divine love going from you to your children. At that time, your children will feel that you have something special to offer.

Of course, when your child smiles, you really do see the presence of God in him. But the moment he screams and does a few

undivine things, at that time do you see God
there? No, you simply say, "This is my fate.
This kind of God I do not want." This moment
you will see something divine and the next
moment you will see only imperfection and say
that God is not there.

But from the spiritual point of view, it is
very important to try to see God inside your
children. When you speak to your children,
you have to feel that you are offering your love
to the Inner Pilot in them. When you are giving
them wisdom, you have to feel that between
you and your children there is somebody who
is a bridge, and that is God. You are loving
your dearest ones precisely because God the
eternal Love is inside you and inside them. You
are showing compassion to them because the
eternally compassionate Source is inside you.

So in all your actions you have to feel that
you are offering your soulful service-light to
the Supreme in your children. Before you feed
your children, think of the Supreme. While
feeding them, say to the Supreme, "O Supreme,
I am offering this food to You." Then, each
time you do something for your children, ask
the Supreme inwardly to do the same for you.
When you feed your children, say to the
Supreme, "You also please feed me, since I am
Your child." At that time the Supreme will
definitely feed you spiritually. And after you
have fed your children, when they are quite
happy and peaceful, pray to the Supreme to
feed you once again. In this way, even though
you are feeding your children only once, the
Supreme is feeding you three times. Why is He

feeding you? Because you are crying for His inner food.

The Supreme should always come first in your life. When your child gives you a smile, do not feel that you have achieved the highest. Instead, feel that you are a child of the Supreme and when *He* smiles at you, when *He* is pleased with you, only then do you get the greatest joy. When you get something from the Supreme, you have to feel that that is the only thing you need. Once you get it, then you can give it to your children, to your husband, to your near and dear ones. Everything that you want to get, try to get from the Supreme, and then give it to your dear ones. If you try to get something from your children, you will only bind yourself.

To gain access to the Supreme and to increase your receptivity to the things that He is offering you, you have to learn concentration, meditation and contemplation. If you are a mother, easily you can find time to meditate, provided you are willing to do first things first. Early in the morning, before your family wakes up and you have to enter into the hustle and bustle of life, you can offer a few seconds to God. If you know that at a particular hour your children will demand food and other things from you, then you can easily get up ten minutes earlier. If you know that at six o'clock they may create problems for you, then you can get up at five-thirty and meditate in secret, like a divine thief.

There is a world of difference between praying and meditating for your children and then taking care of their earthly necessities,

and only taking care of their earthly necessities.
Please do not feel that you are taking proper
care of your children if you are only meeting
with their outer necessities. And please do not
think that if you spend hours with your
children, pleasing them in their own way,
that they will be spiritual. If you want your
children to become spiritual, you yourself have
to be spiritual. You have to pray and meditate
and you have to teach your children how to
pray and meditate. Anything that is good you
have to teach your children. It is also better for
the family to meditate together if it is possible.
Then there will be a real family feeling. As you
eat physical food together, so also you can eat
spiritual food together. Spiritual food is prayer
and meditation.

*Setting a spiritual example*

Children feel that whatever their parents do
is always best, so they often become exactly
like their parents. If the parents like something,
immediately the children like it. If the parents
have some good friends, spiritual friends, the
children immediately become friends with
them. In the beginning, children always try to
imitate their parents. So parents should always
behave extremely well in front of their children.
If the parents misbehave, the children will be
totally ruined. If the parents tell lies or do bad
things, then the children will follow their
parents' example.

Early in the morning, if you get up to pray
and meditate with folded hands, for a few days
your child may remain fast asleep while you

are doing it. But soon a sweet sense of competition will come into him. If his father or his mother can meditate, what is wrong with his doing it? Then the child will sit beside you and meditate. The best example is the parent's own life. The parent's life is the child's ideal.

You can offer your children most effective spiritual help only by leading the divine life yourself—that is to say, by action, not by preaching. Whatever you tell a child to do, you yourself have to do first. You may tell your children, "Get up at seven o'clock and pray and meditate," but the next morning you will be sleeping. Similarly, you may tell your children not to tell lies, but you yourself will tell lies. Everything you do you will justify by saying, "Oh, I have passed your stage; these things don't affect me." But you have to know that they do affect you and they also affect your children.

If you ask your children to get up and meditate and you yourself do the same, automatically they get added strength. But if you don't do the same thing, already half their strength goes away. Their attention is immediately diverted. They think: "If this is really good, how is it that my mother is not doing it?"

Always try to become an example for your children. If you ask your children to draw something and you yourself start cooking, you will be making a mistake. You should not cook at that time; you should go and draw with your children. Even while the children are playing with a ball, although you may feel that you have important things to do, the most important thing for you to do is to keep the children company. There can be nothing more important in your life. If you really want to see their progress, make them happy—not by becoming indulgent, not by giving them twenty toys at a time, but by doing something for them, by giving them the feeling that they are good and divine.

When you are with them, tell them, "God loves you most. You are His chosen child. The whole world is waiting for you to do something divine." This is what I mean by making them happy. To give them real happiness, make them feel that God wants them. This is not insincere flattery. When parents admire and adore a child, even if the qualities that they are admiring are not to the fore, they come to the fore.

In India when a child is born blind, the parents give him the name "Lotus-eyed." They compare the child to the cosmic gods. People may say this is silly, but these parents are doing the right thing by saying that their children have the special grace of the cosmic gods. They are invoking the presence of the cosmic gods. So when you appreciate, admire and adore your children, please try to feel that you are helping them develop the qualities that you feel ought to come to the fore in them; you are bringing to the fore their dormant inner divinity.

It is always good to inspire young children. To inspire them you do not have to paint a big painting or read a beautiful poem. No! Say to them one nice word and immediately they are inspired. Give them a soulful smile or a soulful look and immediately they will see something inside your smile which will inspire them and make their hearts expand.

If you tell a child that he is good, your human mind will say that you have only aggrandised his ego. But your heart will know that immediately the child's heart has expanded. His heart is like a bud that needs to unfold. From each good word and each kind gesture that you offer him, petal by petal the rose or lotus inside the child's heart will blossom. In this way, at every moment you can inspire children with your own way of approaching divinity.

If you can inspire your child with love, then he will inspire somebody else with love. It is from the one that we come to the many. This is the only way the world can progress. When a spiritual Master like the Christ comes, he is only one person; but he inspires millions and millions. We cannot dream of transforming humanity all at once; it is a slow process. But by starting with the children of the world, eventually the face of reality is transformed by divine love.

*Question:* What is the best attitude for bringing up children?

*Sri Chinmoy:* The best attitude for bringing up children is guidance, compassion, forgiveness and conscious oneness.

*Question:* What is a mother's duty in bringing up children?

*Sri Chinmoy:* The mother's duty is to teach the children how to pray, how to be simple, sincere and loving. These are a few things that the mother should take as her bounden duty in bringing up her children.

*Question:* What is the responsibility of the father in bringing up children?

*Sri Chinmoy:* The father's responsibility is to teach his knowledge and wisdom and to bring to the children the message of the vast world. The little family is not all; there is a large family also. The mother will use all her loving, intimate, affectionate qualities. The father will also do that, but the father will also bring the message of the outer world to the children. The mother will make the family sweet, sweeter, sweetest and the father will bring the outer world closer to the children. He will make them feel that there is another world which has to be housed inside the little world, or that the little world has to be part and parcel of that large world.

*Question:* How should parents work together in bringing up children?

*Sri Chinmoy:* Parents should do their respective duties as I mentioned. Whatever the father has to do, the father should do gladly, soulfully, devotedly, untiringly and unconditionally. Whatever the mother has to do, she should also do gladly, soulfully, devotedly, untiringly and unconditionally. This is the only way to bring up children satisfactorily.

*Question:* How can I be a better wife and mother?

*Sri Chinmoy:* You have to feel that inside your husband, inside your son, is God. You love your husband and son not because they are your dearest but because inside them is your Dearest, everybody's Dearest. Inside your family you have to feel the presence of God. If you can vividly see and feel the presence of God inside your near and dear ones, then you will see that you are ready to do everything for them.

Right now, when you do something for your husband or child, sometimes you do it unwillingly. You do it because you feel it is an obligation. But when you do something for God, you will do it with pure joy because when He asks you to do something, He gives you the necessary strength plus the inspiration. So if you can see and feel God's presence inside your husband and son, then you will be able to maintain that same kind of inspiration and joy.

*Question:* Isn't the love between mother and child often possessive?

*Sri Chinmoy:* At the beginning, the mother will not allow her child to be touched by ordinary human beings; only friends, relatives and dear ones are allowed to touch or fondle the child. The mother is reluctant, because she feels that the child is her possession and if they fondle or caress him, perhaps the child will lose his beauty. But what is inside her fear? It is her unillumined love for the child. If her love were absolutely illumined, she would immediately feel, "I am the mother of this child. Let others also appreciate him. He is God's creation and God has given him to me. So let other children of God also appreciate their little brother."

After four or five years, the mother takes the child to kindergarten. Again, she relies on those who have the same love for the child, but now she has a little more illumination. She allows the child to go to school and start learning. Then she allows him to go to high school and college.

For the little child of seven or eight, his whole world is his mother. Love means his mother and nobody else. A few years later, when he is playing and singing with his friends, his feeling of love expands a little. Then, when he studies at school and college, it is his state or his country that he feels love for. Then a day comes when he feels that not only does he belong to a particular country but to the whole world. And then he goes still higher and deeper until finally he feels that he is universal, and his love embraces everything in God's creation. He starts by loving his own physical mother. Then gradually he expands his love to the universal Mother, who embodies the entire creation.

*Question:* Do you feel that having only one parent affects children, and if so, how?

*Sri Chinmoy:* Very often, having only one parent does affect children. Children want to have both a father and a mother. Only then do they feel that the family is complete. But again, in hundreds of cases we have seen that the father can show the children the affection and love of both father and mother, or that the mother has the capacity to offer the love that the children expect from their father as well. If the father is not alive, naturally the mother is expected to offer and bound to offer the father's love as well. And if the mother is not alive, the father has to play the mother's role.

*Question:* What advice can you offer to single parents?

*Sri Chinmoy:* To those who are single parents because of divorce, my only suggestion is that they should not speak ill of the other party to their children. The children should not be influenced. Let the children listen to the dictates of their hearts. Let them feel that both their father and their mother are good. Let their hearts, like magnets, pull the good qualities of the father and of the mother. Neither the father nor the mother should consciously or unconsciously influence the children against the other partner.

Parents should be very careful if they get a divorce. They should pay extra attention to the children, for when the family breaks, the consciousness of the children will break automatically. And who is responsible? The parents are one hundred percent responsible. Therefore, they should take action to rectify the situation to some extent. They can only do so by giving more love, abundant love, and by showing the children that their separation will in no way affect their love for them. What is of paramount importance is love. They have to offer their children boundless love.

*Question:* Can a bad mother make her son great?

*Sri Chinmoy:* It is possible, but it is very difficult. Children are brought up by the mother. In the very beginning, if the mother makes the child feel that he is useless, then he will always feel useless. In most cases, it is the mother's strength that the children get.

*Question:* What if your child is very active and his energy is taking away from your energy? You really can't speak to him, because he doesn't understand, so what can you do to try to calm his vibrations?

*Sri Chinmoy:* Play some spiritual music. If your child is very active, making noise and so on, he will see music as a friend, as somebody to talk to. When he hears spiritual music, you will see him playing with the music. He will feel that he has a friend just beside him, a friend that is as dynamic as he is. So, when the two friends are playing together, then the mother can go into some other room to pray and meditate. Music is the best thing.

*Question:* Whenever I get unhappy, it generally has to do with my attachment, concern and worry about my 14-year-old daughter.

*Sri Chinmoy:* I am answering this question on your daughter's behalf. You should convince yourself that fourteen years ago your daughter didn't exist for you and you also didn't exist for her. And you will go to the other world before her. Your daughter is just like a mango that you have plucked from a mango tree. You will not keep it forever. After sixty or seventy years when she goes back to the Source, you will not be able to claim her. We can claim only those things that are with us permanently.

Do you get any benefit by worrying? No! You only kill yourself and, at the same time, the forces of your worry also enter into her. So this allows more undivine forces to enter into the situation. If you go on worrying too much, this worry itself is an undivine force. If your daughter is not at home and you are worrying about her, then like a bullet your worries enter into her. They will not enter into her as worries but as something else that is unpleasant. She will feel a stomach upset or some other physical disturbance. So when you worry or you are angry, your unhappiness will enter into your daughter in some other form and create unpleasantness for her.

I wish to tell you that you will be happy only on the day you feel that you are not indispensable to your daughter. The Supreme alone is indispensable. The moment you have that feeling, you will have happiness. You are one hundred percent responsible for offering good will to your daughter, who is dearest to your heart. You are under an obligation to offer her good will at every moment. But to worry or to be angry and upset does not help at all.

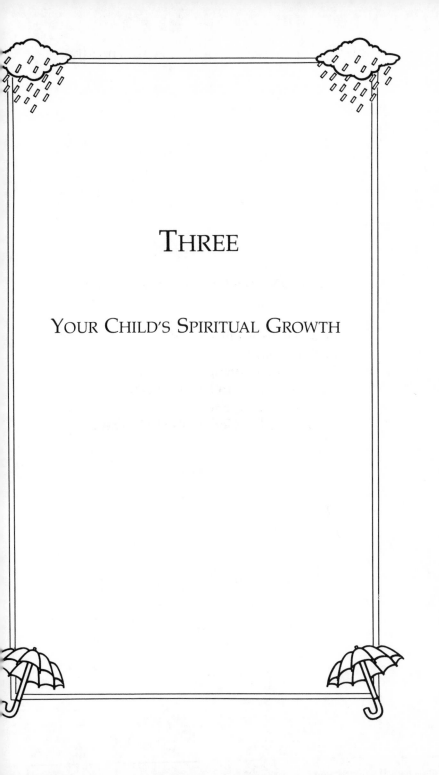

# THREE

## YOUR CHILD'S SPIRITUAL GROWTH

## BE SPONTANEOUS LIKE A CHILD

Be spontaneous like a child.
A child does not try
To acquire anything unnatural.
He does not try to be somebody
    Or something else.
He approaches God in a natural way.

# 3

A child should be taught spirituality from the very first moment he sees the light of day. When the child cries for the first time, the mother must ask herself why the child has cried. Is it because the child saw ignorance-sea for the first time and became afraid, or is it because the child is missing the light and delight which he was wont to enjoy?

If the mother feels that it is ignorance-sea which has frightened the child, then inwardly she must tell the child that this ignorance-sea is short-lived, and that soon he will be swimming in wisdom-sea and enjoying supreme satisfaction. If the mother feels that it is the separation from Heaven-Light that has compelled the child to cry, then inwardly she must tell the child that God is not only in Heaven but also on earth. She must tell the child that God sent him down to earth to fulfil a special purpose. In either case, the mother must speak to the inner reality of the child, which is the soul.

Outwardly, also, you can start a child's spiritual journey at a very tender age—at six months even. Perhaps the child cannot utter a word, but, for example, if you are a Christian

you can show him a picture of the Christ. God
expresses Himself through beauty, so you can
also show the child something beautiful, like a
flower. A child can appreciate the beauty of a
flower. At that time, the flower itself is God for
the child. Then, when the child can speak, let
him say 'God' a few times as his prayer. As he
advances in years, he can be taught higher
meditation.

You give your child the only real freedom
when you give him the truth, the reality. Real
freedom does not lie in striking someone or
moving around like a vagabond. No! Real
freedom lies in doing everything the way God
wants us to do it. That is freedom. God is all
light, all freedom, and if we listen to Him, only
then do we enjoy real freedom.

Sometimes parents ask me how they can describe to a small child something like prayer or
meditation, which they feel is abstract. But for
an adult, prayer and meditation are not
abstract. When we pray, we fold our hands and
cry inwardly to Someone who is above us or
within us. If you want to explain prayer to a
young child, do not try to convince him only
with the physical. Tell him that prayer is something totally different from just folding his
hands and looking up. Tell him that prayer is
something that he has to do inside, but if he
wants to see or feel it, then he has to fold his
hands. You can tell a child that prayer is something which he will feel when he folds his hands
and talks to God. Then, when he folds his
hands and feels something within—whether it is
awe or love or sweetness or softness—then for

him prayer will no longer be abstract; it will be a reality.

For meditation, the child has to sit calmly and quietly. When he sits like that, immediately he will begin to feel that he is meditating. This concrete action will take him into something which originally may seem abstract. You can teach a child through outer action, but do not neglect to emphasise the inner feeling. When he starts feeling joy, peace and love and gradually becomes these things on the strength of his meditation, how can they remain abstract? His body is not abstract to him because he identifies with his body. Whatever he identifies with, he claims as his own. If he identifies himself with prayer or meditation, he will feel peace, joy, love and so on. And once he feels these things, he gives form to them and they no longer remain abstract.

Prayer and meditation are like two roads. Prayer is always done for our own sake, for our own life, for the near and dear ones in our own small world. But meditation is for the entire world. When we meditate well, we feel our oneness with our own expanded reality and fulfil not only ourselves but the entire world. Prayer is necessary and meditation is necessary. When I pray, I talk and my Father listens. When I meditate, my Father talks and I listen. When we pray, we go up to God; when we meditate, God comes down to us. Ultimately it is the same.

Right from childhood, we are taught to pray to God for everything. Our parents teach us to pray, but they do not teach us what to pray for. They say, "Pray to God for everything you want." So we start praying: "O God, please make me be first in the examination"; "O God, let me be first in the running race"; and so on. When we start praying for all these kinds of things, there is no end.

Instead, parents should say to their children, "Pray to God to make your mind calm and quiet so that you will feel peace and bliss everywhere. Pray in the heart." But unfortunately, the parents do not tell this to their children, so from early childhood, children pray for every silly thing. Still, it is certainly better to pray to God for silly things than not to think of God at all.

The better thing is to meditate. If children are taught how to meditate, they will not develop the habit of expecting God to fulfil their desires. You should tell your children, "If you meditate, your mind will be calm and quiet. You will become totally one with the vastness of Infinity and God will become your Friend."

Question: Is a parent responsible for a child's aspiration?

Sri Chinmoy: Yes, parents are always responsible for a child's aspiration. From the very beginning the parents can read the child books about God. The parents can also teach the child to read and give the child spiritual books to read himself. The parents must teach the child how to pray and how to meditate and also see that the child's friends are spiritual.

*Question*: What is the best thing I can give to my child?

*Sri Chinmoy:* The best thing you can give to your child is your daily utterance of the Supreme's Name. Early in the morning repeat "Supreme" seven times in front of your child. Place your hand on his heart lightly and repeat "Supreme" very soulfully. In the evening do it again. This is the best thing.

If the child can speak, then teach the child first and foremost to say "Supreme." If that is done, then the child can start praying. The child will make the fastest progress by following your example. If the parents are praying and meditating together, the child should not be left in another room. The child should observe what the parents are doing. If the parents always do the right thing, the spiritual thing, then the child will imitate them. If the mother drinks milk, immediately the child will drink it. Whatever the child is taught by the parents, he learns. When parents make progress, automatically the child also makes progress.

*Question:* Why do you recommend using the word 'Supreme' as God's Name?

*Sri Chinmoy:* All religious faiths have the same God, but they address Him differently. A man will be called 'Father' by one person, 'Brother' by another and 'Uncle' by another. When he goes to the office, he is called by his surname. When he mixes with his friends, they

will call him by his given name. He is the same
person, but he is addressed in different ways,
according to one's connection with him. Similarly, God is also addressed in various ways,
according to one's sweetest, most affectionate
feeling. Instead of using the word 'God', I use
the word 'Supreme' most of the time, for I feel
it gives us a more intimate connection with
Him.

Usually when we say 'God', we feel that He
embodies a height which is static. We feel that
He has reached His Height and stopped. He
does not have a constantly evolving consciousness. But when we say 'Supreme', we are
speaking of the Supreme Lord who not only
reaches the absolute Height, but all the time
goes beyond, beyond and transcends the
Beyond.

*Question:* When a child asks you, "Who is
God?" what is the best answer to give him?

*Sri Chinmoy:* When you tell a child about
God, do not speak about Him as an old man.
Always make the child feel that God is
somebody of his own age. If the child is three
years old, then God is also three years old for
him. Tell him God is his good Friend, his eternal Friend. Tell him to be prepared for God.
God is coming to him as his most intimate
Friend, so he has to behave well.

But the best answer is to tell the child to look
into a mirror and to smile as soulfully as possible. The word 'soulfully' the child may not
understand, but the child can easily see how

beautiful he looks. Tell the child to try to give absolutely the most beautiful smile and then to look at himself. The child will know whether it is a beautiful smile or just an ordinary smile. The more beautiful the smile, the more his divinity will come forward. An adult may have to pray and meditate and develop a divine consciousness, but a child can do it easily. When the child looks at his most beautiful, glowing consciousness, you tell him that he is seeing God and nobody else.

Who is God? God is our own highest reality. If you can give a soulful smile that will immediately illumine yourself and the whole world, that smile is nothing other than God. Let the child remain in the consciousness of his most beautiful smile, a smile that pervades the length and breadth of the world. For a child, this is the easiest answer for him to understand and also the most effective and convincing answer. And at the same time, it is absolutely true. You are in no way fooling the child.

*Question:* What is the best way to convey to a child what God represents? Should we tell a child that God is love or omniscience or what?

*Sri Chinmoy:* We know that God is everything, God is inside everything and God is beyond everything. This is our philosophical understanding and our psychic understanding. But I wish to speak about God from a child's pure, innocent and soulful point of view— according to a child's understanding.

What is God from the point of view of a child? God is concern. A mother will try to show her concern for her child day in and day out. But out of twenty-four hours, the mother can consciously offer her concern for only two or three hours in spite of her best intentions. She wants to show him all her affection all the time. But during the day she has to study or work, do her own meditation and do quite a few other things apart from taking care of him—even though he is her dearest child. When he is sick, perhaps she will offer her concern for fifteen or sixteen or even twenty-four hours. Ordinarily she can give him her concern for only a few hours. In God's case, it is different. He constantly gives us His inner and outer Concern.

We stay on earth for fifty, sixty, seventy or even one hundred years, but this is not our real span of life. Our real life is endless. We came from the beginningless past and we are entering into the endless future. We have had previous incarnations and we will have many future incarnations. In our past incarnations we had different parents. In this incarnation we get concern from one mother and father; in our previous incarnation we got concern from other parents and in the future also we will receive concern from different parents. But we received God's Concern from the very beginning and forever it will remain the same. The moment He created our soul, His Concern started, and it will always remain constant and eternal.

Everything has a source, and the source of concern is oneness. When my finger is hurt or bleeding, immediately I am concerned for my finger. Why? Because I am one with my finger. When something is wrong with your child, you show your concern because of your oneness with him. Right now, there are many people who are suffering and dying in the hospital, but even if you knew them you might not offer them your concern. Why? Because you are not completely identified with them and you don't feel your oneness with them. But you do feel your oneness with your child and your child feels his oneness with you. So we see that the source of concern is oneness. It is to your near and dear ones, those who you feel are part and parcel of your life, that you offer your concern. Since God is the all-pervading One, His Concern comes from His all-pervading Oneness. Since He is everywhere and in everything, He has to have oneness with everything. So He offers everything His Concern.

# FOUR

## A PARENT'S GUIDE TO MEDITATION

TWO  PURPOSES


God created you for only two purposes:
One is to be true to Him
And the other is to be true to yourself.

# 4

MEDITATION is the language of God. When you and I speak English, we are able to understand one another. If you want to communicate with God, then meditation is the language that you must speak. It is the common language of man and God. God uses it and man uses it. When you go deep within, into the deepest recesses of your heart, you commune with God through meditation.

Thinking has nothing to do with meditation. Even reflection, which is a quiet kind of introspective thinking, is far from the disciplined vastness of meditation. The moment you start thinking, you play with limitation and bondage. Your thoughts, no matter how sweet or delicious at the moment, are painful, venomous and destructive in the long run because they limit and bind you. In the thinking mind there is no reality. One moment you are building a castle and the following moment you are breaking it. The mind has its purpose, but in the spiritual life you have to go far above the mind

Excerpted from the book *Meditation: Man-Perfection in God-Satisfaction* by Sri Chinmoy.

where there is eternal peace, eternal knowledge and eternal light. When you go beyond thinking with the help of your aspiration and meditation, only then can you see and enjoy God's Reality and God's Vision together.

*Starting out*

When you start meditating, try always to feel that you are a child. When one is a child, one's mind is not developed. At the age of twelve or thirteen, the mind starts functioning on an intellectual level. But before that, a child is all heart. A child feels that he does not know anything. He does not have any preconceived ideas about meditation and the spiritual life. He wants to learn everything fresh from the mother or the father.

First feel that you are a child, and then try to feel that you are standing in a flower garden. This flower garden is your heart. A child can play in a garden for hours. He goes from this flower to that flower, but he does not leave the garden because he gets joy from the beauty and fragrance of each flower. Inside you is a garden, and you can stay in it for as long as you want and learn to meditate there.

If you can remain in your heart, you will begin to feel an inner cry. This inner cry, which is aspiration, is the secret of meditation. When a grown-up person cries, his cry is usually not sincere. But when a child cries, even if he is crying only for candy, he is very sincere. At that time, candy is the whole world for him. If you give him a hundred-dollar bill, he will not be satisfied; he cares only for candy. Now, what happens when a child cries? Immediately his father or mother comes to help him. If you can cry from deep within for peace, light and truth, and if this is the only thing that will satisfy you, then God your eternal Father and eternal Mother is bound to come and help you.

*Spiritual exercises*

There are quite a few exercises that a beginner can practice. For a spiritual seeker, simplicity, sincerity, purity and surety are of utmost importance. It is simplicity that grants you peace of mind. It is sincerity that makes you feel that you are of God and that God is constantly for you. It is your pure heart that can make you feel at every moment that God is growing and glowing and fulfilling Himself inside you. It is surety that makes you feel that meditation is absolutely the right thing.

In silence kindly repeat the world 'simplicity' inside your mind seven times and concentrate on the crown of your head. Then repeat the word 'sincerity' seven times silently and soulfully inside your heart and concentrate on your heart. Then kindly repeat the word 'purity' seven times inside or around your navel centre and concentrate on the navel centre. Please do it silently and most soulfully. Then focus your attention on the third eye, which is between and slightly above the eyebrows, and silently repeat 'surety' seven times. Next, place your hand on top of your head and say three times, "I am simple, I am simple, I am simple." Then place your hand on your heart and say three times, "I am sincere, I am sincere." Then do it on the navel centre, saying, "I am pure," and on the third eye, repeating, "I am sure."

Now, if you prefer a particular aspect of God —love, for instance—please inwardly repeat the word 'love' most soulfully several times. While uttering the word 'love' most soulfully, try to feel that it is reverberating in the inmost recesses of your heart: "Love, love, love." If you care more for divine peace, then please inwardly chant or repeat to yourself the word 'peace'. While doing this, try to hear the cosmic sound that the word embodies. Feel that 'peace' is a seed-sound reverberating in the very depths of your heart. If you want light, then please repeat, "Light, light, light," most soulfully and feel that you have actually become light. From the soles of your feet to the crown of your head, try to feel that you have become the word that you are repeating. Feel that your physical body, subtle body and all your nerves are flooded with love or peace or light.

There is one other thing that you can try. Please breathe in and hold your breath for a couple of seconds, and feel that you are holding the breath, or life-energy, in the third eye. This is where your concentration will be. The second time you breathe in, hold the life-energy in the heart centre. And the third time you breathe in, hold the breath in the navel centre. This will also help you.

A child does not depend or rely on himself; he depends only on his mother's capacity. Again, he is eager to give her what little capacity he has. His little capacity is his faith. His faith in his mother is his faith in himself. If a child is lost in the street and he begins to cry, some kind-hearted person will show him where his home is. Feel that you are lost in the street and that there is a storm raging outside. Doubt, fear, anxiety, worry, insecurity and other undivine forces are pouring down on you. But if you feel that you are helpless and cry sincerely, Somebody will come to rescue you and show you how to get to your home, which is your heart. And who is that Somebody? It is God, your Inner Pilot.

Each person's soul has its own way of meditating. My way of meditating will not suit you, and your way of meditating will not suit me. There are many seekers whose meditation is not fruitful because they are not doing the meditation that is right for them. If you don't have a spiritual Master who can guide you, then you have to go deep within and get your meditation from the inmost recesses of your heart. Go deep, deep within and see if you get a voice or thought or idea. Then, go deep into this voice or thought and see if it gives you a feeling of inner joy or peace, where there are no questions or problems or doubts. When you get this kind of feeling, then you can know that the voice that you have heard is the real inner voice which will help you in your spiritual life.

In the very beginning you should not even think about meditation. Just try to set aside a certain time of day when you will be calm and quiet, and feel that these five minutes belong to your inner being and nobody else. What you need is regular practice at a regular time. Every day you eat; that is how you live on earth. You cannot live on the food you ate yesterday. Similarly, every day you have to feed the soul.

If you eat every day, you become very strong because of your regular nourishment. So also when you meditate every day, your soul is being nourished.

*Preparing to meditate*

When you meditate at home, you should have a corner of your room which is absolutely pure and sanctified—a sacred place which you use only for meditation. Here on your shrine you will keep a picture of your spiritual Master, or the Christ, or some other beloved spiritual figure whom you regard as your Master.

Before beginning to meditate, it is helpful if you can take a shower or proper bath. The purification of the body is absolutely necessary for the purification of the consciousness. If you are unable to take a shower or bath before sitting down to meditate, you should at least wash your face and your feet. It is also advisable to wear clean and light clothes.

It will help if you burn incense and keep some flowers in front of you. There are some people who say that it is not necessary to have flowers around during meditation. They say, "The flower is inside; the thousand-petalled lotus is inside." But the physical flower that you have in front of you reminds you of the inner flower. Its colour, its fragrance and its pure consciousness can give you a little inspiration. From inspiration you get aspiration, and from aspiration you get realisation.

It is the same with using candles during meditation. The flame from a candle will not in itself give you aspiration; it is the inner flame that will give you aspiration. But when you see the outer flame, then immediately you feel that the flame in your inner being is also climbing high, higher, highest. And when you smell the scent of incense, you get perhaps only an iota of inspiration and purification, but this iota can be added to your inner treasure.

When meditating, it is important to keep the spine straight and erect, and to keep the body relaxed. When the body is stiff, naturally the divine and fulfilling qualities that are flowing in and through it during meditation will not be received. The body should not be uncomfortable either. When it feels uncomfortable, automatically it will change its position. While you are meditating, your inner being will spontaneously take you to a comfortable position, and then it is up to you to maintain it. The main advantage of the lotus position is that it helps keep the spinal cord straight and erect. But it will not necessarily keep the body relaxed. So the lotus position is not at all necessary for proper meditation. Many people meditate very well while they are seated in a chair.

Some people do physical exercises and postures. These exercises, called hatha yoga, relax the body and bring peace of mind for a short period. If someone is physically very restless and cannot stay still for more than a second, then these exercises will definitely help. But hatha yoga is not at all necessary. There are many aspirants who can just sit and make their minds calm and quiet without doing any hatha yoga.

*Proper breathing*

Proper breathing is very important in meditation. When breathing, try to breathe in as slowly and quietly as possible, so that if somebody placed a tiny thread in front of your nose it would not move at all. And when you breathe out, try to breathe out even more slowly than when you breathed in. If possible, leave a short pause between the end of your first exhalation and the beginning of your second inhalation. If you can, hold your breath for a few seconds. But if it is difficult, do not do it. Never do anything that will harm your organs or respiratory system.

The first thing that you have to think of when breathing is purity. When you breathe in, it you can feel that the breath is coming directly from God, from Purity itself, then your breath can easily be purified. Then each time you breathe in, try to feel that you are bringing into your body peace, infinite peace. The opposite of peace is restlessness. When you breathe out, try to feel that you are expelling the restlessness within you and also the restlessness that you see all around you. When you breathe this way, you will find restlessness leaving you. After practising this for a few times, please try to feel that you are breathing in power from the universe. And when you exhale, feel that all your fear is coming out of your body. After doing this a few times, try to feel that what you are breathing in is joy, infinite joy, and what you are breathing out is sorrow, suffering and melancholy.

There is another thing that you can also try. Feel that you are breathing in not air but cosmic energy. Feel that tremendous cosmic energy is entering into you with each breath and that you are going to use it to purify your body, vital, mind and heart. Feel that there is not a single place in your body that is not being occupied by the flow of cosmic energy. It is flowing like a river inside you, washing and purifying your whole being. Then, when you start to breathe out, feel that you are breathing out all the rubbish inside you—all your undivine thoughts, obscure ideas and impure actions. Anything inside your system that you call undivine, anything that you do not want to claim as your own, feel that you are exhaling.

## Concentration

If you are just beginning to meditate, start by developing the power of concentration. Otherwise, the moment you try to make your mind calm and vacant, millions of uncomely thoughts will enter into you and you will not be able to meditate even for one second. If you can concentrate for a few minutes each day before entering into meditation, it clears away obstacles and helps you make rapid progress.

Concentration means inner vigilance and alertness. When we concentrate, we are like a bullet entering into something or we are like a magnet pulling the object of concentration toward us. At that time, we do not allow any thought to enter into our mind, whether it is good or bad. In concentration the entire mind has to be focused on a particular object or sub-

ject. If we are concentrating on a flower, we try
to feel that nothing else exists in the entire
world but ourself and the flower. Concentration is not an aggressive way of looking into an
object. Far from it! This concentration comes
directly from the soul, from the soul's indomi-
table will power.

Very often I hear aspirants say that they
cannot concentrate for more than five minutes.
After five minutes they get a headache or their
head is on fire. Why? It is because the power of
their concentration is coming from the intellectual mind, or, you can say, from the disciplined
mind. The mind knows that it must not
wander; that much knowledge the mind has.
But if the mind is to be utilised properly, in an
illumined way, then the light of the soul has to
come into it. When the light of the soul has
entered into the mind, it is extremely easy to
concentrate on something for hours and hours.
During this time there can be no thoughts or
doubts or fears. No negative forces can enter
into the mind if it is surcharged with the soul's
light.

When you concentrate, you have to feel that
your power of concentration is coming from
the heart centre and then going up to the third
eye. The heart centre is where the soul is
located. When you think of the soul at this
time, it is better not to form any specific idea of
it or try to think of what it looks like. Only
you will think of it as God's representative or
as boundless light and delight. So when you
concentrate, you try to feel that the soul's light
is coming from the heart and passing through
the third eye. Then, with this light, you enter

into the object of concentration and identify
with it. The final stage of concentration is to
discover the hidden ultimate truth in the object
of concentration.

## Conquering thoughts

Now let us come to the problem of thoughts.
The moment an undivine thought or wrong
thought enters into your mind, your aspiration
must cut it to pieces, because during meditation
everything is intense. While you are talking or
engaging in your ordinary earthly activities,
you can have any kind of thought, for your
thoughts are not intense at those times. But
during meditation, if any undivine thought
comes, the power of your meditation enlarges
and intensifies it, and it ruins part of your subtle being. Your spiritual life grows weaker the
moment your mind becomes a prey to self-
indulgent thoughts. If a good thought comes,
try to enlarge it as much as possible. If the
good thoughts are on a lower level, you can try
to lift them up to a higher level. But if you have
a bad thought, just cut it off and kill it.

How will you do this? If the thought that is
attacking you is coming from the outer world,
try to muster your soul's will from your heart
and bring it right in front of your forehead.
The moment your soul's will is seen by the
thought which is trying to enter into you, that
thought is bound to disappear.

There is something practical you can do if
you are bothered by thoughts during your
meditation. Please feel that inside your mind
there is a room and also a door. Stand either

inside the room or outside the room, just in front of the door, and wait there to see who is coming. As soon as you see that some people are coming—'people' here means thoughts—you just keep the door closed. In the beginning, in order to become strong, you do not allow anybody in. Otherwise, while you are allowing friends to come in, your enemies may also come in and then you will be totally lost. But there will come a time when you will become inwardly strong and will be in a position to let only your friends come in. At that time you will allow your friends in and keep your enemies outside.

Good thoughts are your friends. Thoughts about God, about self-sacrifice, are good thoughts. When these good thoughts want to enter into your room, you will just leave the door open. But as soon as you see bad thoughts like fear, jealousy, doubt, frustration, depression and so on, you will keep the door closed.

One method of meditation you can use, particularly if your mind is restless, is called "mantra." You can repeat "Supreme" or "God" for a few minutes. Usually it is best to chant a mantra out loud. Just say it in a normal but soulful way.

After doing this for a few minutes, if you can feel that there is somebody inside, your inner being, who is repeating the mantra for you, then you do not have to chant out loud. Sometimes you may have this experience after you have finished. You have repeated "Supreme, Supreme" quite a few times. Then, when you stop, you hear God's Name being repeated inside your heart. Your mouth is not function-

ing; it is your inner being that has started repeating God's Name inside you.

## Meditating in the heart

I always tell seekers that it is better to
meditate in the heart than in the mind. The
mind is like Times Square on New Year's Eve;
the heart is like a lonely cave in the Himalayas.
If you meditate in the mind, you will be able to
meditate for perhaps five minutes; and out of
that five minutes, for one minute you may
meditate powerfully. After that you will feel
your whole head getting tense. First you get joy
and satisfaction, then you may feel a barren
desert. But if you meditate in the heart, you
acquire the capacity to identify yourself with
the joy and satisfaction that you get, and then
it becomes yours permanently.

If you meditate in the mind, you don't
identify; you try to enter into something.
When you want to enter into somebody else's
house to get what that person has, either you
have to break down the door or you have to
plead with the owner of the house to open the
door. When you plead, you feel that you are a
stranger and the owner of the house also feels
that you are a stranger. Then he thinks, "Oh, a
stranger wants to come into my house." But if
you use the heart, immediately the heart's
qualities of softness, sweetness, love and purity
come to the fore. When the owner of the house
sees that you are all heart, immediately his own
heart will become one with yours and he will
let you in. He will feel your oneness with him
and say, "All right, what do you want from my

house? If you need peace, then take it. If you need light, then take it."

If you meditate in the heart, you are meditating where the soul is. True, the light and consciousness of the soul permeate the whole body, but there is a specific place where the soul resides most of the time, and that is in the heart. If you want illumination, you have to get it from the soul, which is inside the heart. When you know what you want and where to find it, the sensible thing is to go to that place. Otherwise, it is like going to the hardware store to get groceries.

Meditation is like going to the bottom of the sea, where everything is calm and tranquil. On the surface there may be a multitude of waves, but the sea is not affected below. In its deepest depths, the sea is all silence. When we start meditating, first we try to reach our own inner existence—that is to say, the bottom of the sea. Then, when the waves come from the outside world, we are not affected. Fear, doubt, worry and all the earthly turmoils will just wash away, because inside us is solid peace. Thoughts cannot touch us, because our mind is all peace, all silence, all oneness. Like fish in the sea, they jump and swim but leave no mark. So when we are in our highest meditation we feel that we are the sea, and the animals in the sea cannot affect us. We feel that we are the sky, and all the birds flying past cannot affect us. Our mind is the sky and our heart is the infinite sea. This is meditation.

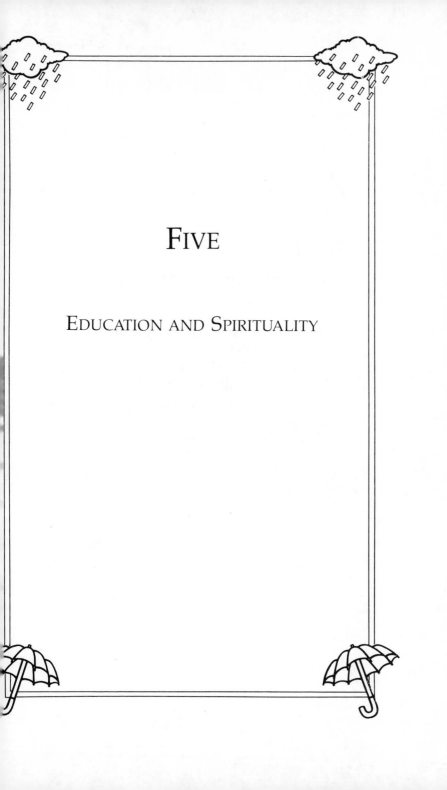

# FIVE

## EDUCATION AND SPIRITUALITY

## JUST FEEL THAT I AM YOURS

The schoolteacher tells his students:
Read, you will know.
The spiritual Teacher tells his students:
Become, you will know.
God tells His eternal students:
Just feel that I am yours.
What more do you need to know?

# 5

QUESTION: From the spiritual point of view, what is education?

*Sri Chinmoy:* There are three kinds of education: human education, divine education and God-education. Human education means keeping our eyes wide open. In order to do that, we must stop making friends with ignorance-night.

Divine education is self-giving. In order to do that, we must feel that God is the only existence-reality both here on earth and there in Heaven.

God-education is satisfaction in perfection. This satisfaction in perfection can be achieved only when we feel that there can be no other way to make ourselves happy than by making God Himself happy.

*Question:* What is the parents' responsibility for the formal education of the children?

*Sri Chinmoy:* The parents have to take full responsibility for the formal education of the children. They have to send the children to school. They have to give proper attention to

their children's studies, to their outer behaviour
and to their inner growth. Children must not be
left alone. At every moment the parents should
take considerable interest in the children's wel-
fare. In the formative years, the parents must
play a most significant role. Children are like
tiny saplings or plants. They have to be shel-
tered and taken proper care of by the parents
until they have grown into large and strong
trees.

*Question:* How can the outer education and
the inner education go hand in hand?

*Sri Chinmoy:* The outer education and the
inner education can go hand in hand provided
one knows what the outer education is and
what the inner education is. The outer
education is concern for humanity. The inner
education is oneness with humanity. If there is
no concern, there can be no oneness. But if
there is oneness, then concern is automatically
there.

*Question:* Were teachers better in the olden
days?

*Sri Chinmoy:* Yes. In the olden days,
especially in the Vedic era, the teachers used to
consider their students as true members of their
immediate family. Therefore, the teachers
shared their wisdom-light constantly and
unreservedly and imparted to their students the
supreme knowledge: *"Tat twam asi.* Thou art

That, That thou art. In essence and substance, my children, you are the One without a second." The teachers of the hoary past not only inspired their students but also aspired in and through them to help them see the effulgence of their own inner sun. This is the sun that illumines the darkness of millennia and transforms truth-experience-possibility into truth-realisation-inevitability.

*Question:* Is it necessary for the parents, teacher and child to be spiritual friends when the child is learning in a particular class?

*Sri Chinmoy:* Yes, it is absolutely necessary for the parent, the teacher and the child to be friends. The parents, the teacher and the child must all feel that they belong to the same family. The parents were the child's first friends. Then his teacher came to him as a friend. The more friends that the child has, the easier it will be for him to conquer his enemy: ignorance. So when he gets more friends, new friends, he must always welcome them.

*Question:* How do we know if we have too much education?

*Sri Chinmoy:* We can know that we have too much or a disproportionate amount of education when we use our earthbound mind-information to exhibit our dazzling capacities or to destroy the spontaneous possibilities in aspiring human souls.

*Question:* How can I best serve the Supreme
in the children that I teach?

*Sri Chinmoy:* You can best serve the
Supreme in the children when you feel
extremely grateful to Him for giving you the
opportunity to teach them. When you teach
children, you are given the opportunity to
become a child yourself. In the spiritual life
your aim is to become a child, an eternal child,
so that you can make constant progress. If you
are constantly grateful to the Supreme, and if
the children remind you of your eternal
childhood, then you will make the fastest
progress.

When you teach children, do not think that
you are serving them because the school
authorities are paying you. No, feel that you
are serving the children because you want to
become another child. If the children offer you
a smile, feel that that smile comes from the
Supreme. Each time a child smiles, it is the
expansion of God's Dream-Reality on earth. If
you remember that, then you will be able to
serve the Supreme most soulfully and constantly.

*Question:* What should I meditate on before
I enter a classroom to teach?

*Sri Chinmoy:* Please meditate on the Supreme
in each student of yours. You do not have to
meditate on each student individually, but try
to feel them all as a single being meditating
right in front of you. When you feel the presence of the Supreme inside the students, please

feel that the Supreme in them is learning from the Supreme within you. You have to feel that the Supreme within you is the elder brother. If the elder brother teaches the younger ones, slowly and steadily they will get his wisdom. If you can do this, then you will be able to see that the students are part and parcel of your own existence.

*Question:* Is there a particular spiritual quality that we should invoke while teaching our children?

*Sri Chinmoy:* There are many qualities that you should invoke while teaching your children, but the most important quality is self-giving. This unparalleled quality you should invoke not only while you are teaching your children but all the time, whether your children are around you or not.

*Question:* How can one teach meditation to young schoolchildren while still obeying the laws which say you can't teach religion?

*Sri Chinmoy:* You have to explain to the school authorities that meditation is not religion; far from it. Religion deals with the physical plane, the vital plane and the mental plane, whereas meditation does not deal with these planes. Meditation deals only with the oneness-plane.

As long as we remain in the physical, vital and mental planes, we shall have differences. We shall have confusing, binding ideas. But if we remain in the world of meditation, which is oneness-reality with God's entire creation, then we far transcend the barriers of religion.

Young students must be taught that meditation does not claim that any religion is superior to others. It does not feed the superiority or inferiority of any religion. Meditation feeds only the individuals who cry for God-manifestation and all-loving self-expansion.

*Question:* How can a teacher know when to be compassionate and when to be a disciplinarian?

*Sri Chinmoy:* There are two roads that lead to the same destination. One road is known as the compassion-road and the other road is known as the discipline-road. Although both roads lead to the same destination, God prefers the compassion-road over the discipline-road for He feels that if a child walks along the compassion-road, then the child will be able to walk much faster.

Only when everything else fails does God resort to disciplining the lives of His students. But again, God tells us that even His disciplinary action is nothing short of compassion, for it is His compassionate Heart which makes Him want to illumine and perfect His children.

Compassion is the first and foremost approach in dealing with unruly children. Discipline is the last resort. Again, on the practical level, the teacher must observe secretly whether a particular student responds more to life's compassionate aspect or to life's disciplinary aspect. By knowing that, he can easily do the needful.

*Question:* Do twins learn in the same way?

*Sri Chinmoy:* Twins need not and cannot learn in the same way, precisely because they have different souls. Each soul has a special way of receiving light from above and manifesting this light on earth. Twins may enter into the earth-arena together, but the promises that they made to the Absolute Supreme while they were in the soul's world may not be the same. Therefore, their ways of learning here on earth and their ways of sharing their knowledge may widely differ.

*Question:* I am a student. How can I study and still keep God before me?

*Sri Chinmoy:* It is very easy. If you study in order to get a diploma so that you will be recognised by everyone, if you study to become the wisest person on earth so that you can teach the world, then it is impossible for you to keep God before you. If you feel that you want a degree for name and fame, for your own establishment on earth, then you cannot keep God before you.

You have to feel that you are studying just because you feel the necessity of pleasing God, just because God wants you to study. You have to feel all the time that you are studying not to please yourself or the members of your family, but only to please God. Feel that God is like a mother watching her child study. While pleasing God, you are pleasing your parents, you are pleasing your relatives, you are pleasing your own self. But God should come first.

You have to take your study as a form of service to God. If you study well and get good marks because you feel that this is your service to God, then you are pleasing God. Today He wants you to study. Tomorrow when you complete your course, God will ask you inwardly to do some other job. The day after tomorrow He may ask you to do something else. So in each field you have to please God in His own way.

Studying is not an obstruction on the spiritual path. You have to discipline yourself to study six, seven, eight hours a day. In a few years' time, the inner capacity and discipline that you have acquired by studying, you will be able to apply to your spiritual life. Discipline in any walk of life has to be appreciated and admired because it is a type of strength. With this strength, God will ask you to build or to break something. If you have strength in your arms, you can lift up a heavy weight. If something has to be broken, you can break it; and if something has to be lifted, you can do that too.

*Question:* How can one see and feel beauty in one's school work?

*Sri Chinmoy:* School work and other work must be taken as a part of our self-discipline. The result of self-discipline is satisfaction. If we care for satisfaction, we have to feel that inside our self-discipline there is nothing but the revealing light of beauty.

# PART TWO

# . . . AND FOR CHILDREN

I have hundreds of friends. Most of them are grown-up people. But I treasure the company of the children much more than I treasure the company of my grown-up friends. Why? Because they are all heart; they are all joy.

To the children I offer this message:

My young friends, do you know that there is a Person who loves you infinitely more than your best friend loves you? Do you want to know His Name? His Name is God.

Do you know there is a Person who loves you infinitely more than your dear parents love you? Do you want to know His Name? His Name is God.

Do you know there is a Person who loves you infinitely more than you love yourselves? Do you want to know His Name? His Name is God.

Do you want me to prove it? It is very easy to prove. Your best friend never feels that you are as great as God. But God always feels that you are as great as He is.

Your parents never feel that you are as good as God. But God always feels that you are as good as He is.

You never knew that you are another God. But God knows that you are another God and He always tells you that very thing. But in order to hear His Voice, you have to pray lovingly every morning and every evening. Please ask your parents to teach you how to pray. If you pray daily, I assure you one day you will hear God's Voice. And then what I have just told you, you yourselves will be able to hear directly from God.

*—Sri Chinmoy*

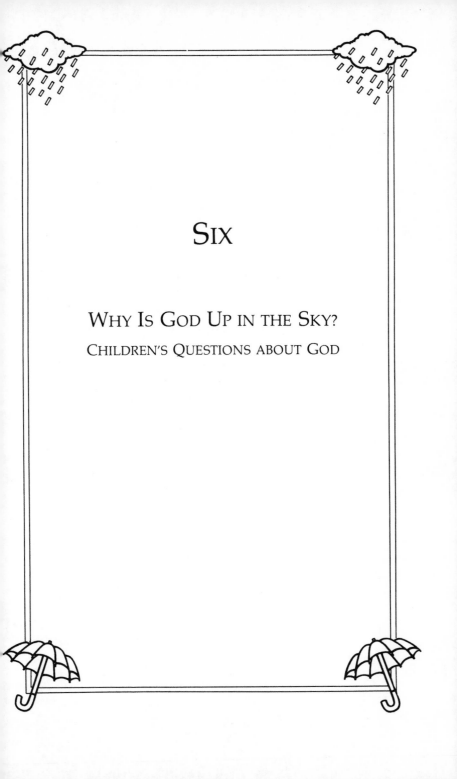

# Six

## Why Is God Up in the Sky?
### Children's Questions about God

# A CHILD'S QUESTION

A child's question
Can be answered in one sentence.
    The same question
Asked by an adult
Requires a thesis as an answer.

# 6

QUESTION: What does God look like?

Sri Chinmoy: God looks exactly like us. In your case, when you see God, He will look exactly like you. When somebody else sees God, God will look exactly like that individual. When any member of your family sees God, He will look exactly like that particular person. As soon as you see God, you will say, "He looks like me!" God's Eyes, His Face, everything of His will look the same as you. The only difference will be that He is infinitely more beautiful than you. That is because your own most illumined part is infinitely more beautiful than your least illumined part. Although you will be able to recognise Him and claim Him as your very own, somebody else may not be able to recognise Him because He has come to you and nobody else.

Question: Why can't I see God inside me?

Sri Chinmoy: You *can* see God inside you. But you can't see Him right now because you

are not crying and trying to see Him. If you
don't ask for something from your mother, she
won't give you anything. If you do ask for
something, your mother will always give it to
you. So if you want to see God, it is best to
look for Him. If you look for Him, then only
will you see Him.

God is like the most beautiful jewel that is
inside your heart-room. If you search for it,
then immediately you will find it. Do not just
look quickly into your room and say that God
is not there. Try to feel that He is there. Once
you really look for Him, definitely you will see
Him.

*Question:* Why is it that I cannot see God?

*Sri Chinmoy:* You do see God but you do
not recognise Him. There are many people on
earth whom you see, but you do not know who
they are. But once somebody tells you who these
people are, then later on when you see them,
easily you can recognise them. For example,
when you saw a policeman for the first time,
you did not know what he was. But once your
parents told you, the next time you saw a
policeman you knew what he was. Similarly,
when you see God, one day either your soul or
your Guru will tell you who God is.

*Question:* How can I be with God?

*Sri Chinmoy:* You can be with God. As a
matter of fact you are always with God. But

you have to be consciously with God. That is to say that when God is in front of you or inside your heart, you have to recognise God. Only if you pray to Him with folded hands, in front of your shrine, early in the morning and also in the evening, can you become one with God.

*Question:* How does God know everything about me?

*Sri Chinmoy:* God knows everything about you because He has created you. When you do something, you know everything you have done because it is you who have done it. If you have drawn a picture, you will know from the very beginning what you have done; therefore, if I ask you how you have done it, you will be able to tell me everything in detail. Similarly, God has created you. Since He has created you, He is bound to know everything about you.

*Question:* How can I see God when I die? How can I see God when I'm alive?

*Sri Chinmoy:* You can see God when you are alive if you pray and meditate most devotedly and soulfully. When you die, it is not *you* who dies. Your body dies, but your soul remains alive and always alert. At that time you are nothing but your soul. Now you are nothing but your body. When you are the

body, you have to pray and meditate to see
God. When you are the soul, you just spread
your wings. Lo, you will see that God also has
wings.

*Question:* Where does God live?

*Sri Chinmoy:* God is everywhere, but He
can most easily be found in your heart-room.
You spend most of your time in your living
room. When somebody wants to see you, he
enters into the living room and finds you there.
Similarly, God spends most of the time in the
heart-room. If you enter into the heart-room,
you will find God there very easily. True, He is
everywhere, but inside the heart-room His
presence is seen and felt most powerfully.

*Question:* I can feel God in my heart, but
how come I can't explain Him?

*Sri Chinmoy:* God is self-explanatory. That
is why you can't explain Him. God needs no
explanation. God spontaneously reveals and
explains Himself. Therefore, He needs no explanation.

*Question:* Why is God up in the sky and not
on earth?

*Sri Chinmoy:* God is up in the sky and He is
also on earth. It is the books you have read
about God, especially in the Western world,

and your parents that have taught you that God is up in the sky. I wish to say that God is up in the sky, but He is also here on earth. If you read the inner book inside your heart, then you will see that God is also on earth. Since you are on earth, although God is all-pervading, the God-consciousness on earth is infinitely more important for you than God who is in the sky, in Heaven.

Now, what is your sky and what is your earth? Your sky is your head and your earth is your feet. When you think of the sky, think of your head, where God is; and when you think of earth, think of your feet, where God also is. You need both your feet and your head. If you don't have your feet, you can't walk. If you don't have a head, then you will have no brain. Both are necessary, although God is in each. Your head is at one place and your feet are at a another place. What connects them is your heart. The heart is the connecting link, the bridge. When you want to see God who is in your head, you can easily go from your feet to your head by crossing the connecting link, which is your heart.

*Question:* What is Heaven?

*Sri Chinmoy:* Heaven is where you get joy and love in boundless measure. Heaven is inside your soul. Where is your soul? Your soul is inside your heart. Where is your heart? Your heart is inside your body.

*Question:* Am I going to God?

*Sri Chinmoy:* Certainly you are going to God. You came from God and you are going back to God. You came from God to earth with a special message: to tell each and everyone in the world how nice, kind, good and beautiful God is. And once you have told what you have to say about God, you will go back to God in Heaven.

*Question:* Will my mother go to Heaven when she dies?

*Sri Chinmoy:* Certainly your mother will go to Heaven when she dies. She will go to take rest and enjoy peace, light and bliss. You will also do the same when you die.

*Question:* Why did God create earth?

*Sri Chinmoy:* God created earth to manifest Himself in human bodies, in human form. Manifestation means His presence—His Beauty, Light, Love, Joy, Concern and Compassion.

*Question:* Why are my teachers in school always so mean?

*Sri Chinmoy:* Sweet boy, I feel sorry for you. At the same time, I also feel sorry for your teachers. You feel that your teachers are always mean. The teachers feel that you

children are always unruly and undisciplined.
The teachers do love you, but right now they
deal with you in a way that is familiar to you:
by shouting and yelling. They feel that this is
the best way, since you are familiar with this
way.

But there is another way, and your teachers
are eager to show you that way. The moment
you become calm, quiet and obedient, your
teachers will give you a soulful smile and their
fruitful wisdom lovingly, steadily and completely.


*Question:* Can I go live with God instead of
with my mother and father?

*Sri Chinmoy:* Yes, you can live with God
instead of with your mother and father.
Although God is in Heaven, He is also on earth
in the form of your father and in the form of
your mother. He feels that if you live here on
earth with your parents, you are staying with
Him. He has two houses. He wants you to stay
in His house on earth, where your parents are.
The other house He is still building; it is not
yet complete. When His house is complete,
then God will ask you to live in that house.


*Question:* How was the first man born on
earth?

*Sri Chinmoy:* The first man was born on
earth by God's Will, God's Will Power. If you
read the Bible you will learn the story of Adam

and Eve. But if you read your inner life story, then you will know how God created the first human being and whom God created first on earth. The first human being was born by God's Will through the evolutionary process, through the continuous and gradual progress of the animal kingdom.

*Question:* On the path to God, what is purity and what is realisation?

*Sri Chinmoy:* On the path to God, purity is the fragrance of a flower and realisation is the flower. Both are equally important. If you don't have fragrance, then the flower is useless. If you do not have a flower, how can you have fragrance? So both flower and fragrance are of equal importance. If you feel the presence of a flower inside your heart and if you also smell the fragrance, then you will be able to reach your destined goal without fail.

*Question:* Why isn't God a human being like us?

*Sri Chinmoy:* God is definitely a human being like us. Unfortunately, we do not recognise Him. Why do we not recognise Him as a human being? Because we do not use the special eye and special heart that are inside us. This special eye is between our two ordinary eyes and a little above. The spiritual heart is inside our ordinary heart. Once that special eye and special heart are opened, then we will easily be able to see that like us, He is a human being.

*Question:* Why is it that some people see light and others don't?

*Sri Chinmoy:* Some people see light and others don't because some people need light while others don't need it. If you need something, then you see it, get it and grow into it. If you don't need it, you will not care to see it. When you were a baby, you cried for toys and your parents did give you toys. Now you are a little bit grown up. You do not care for toys as much as you did before. Therefore, your parents do not bring you the same number of toys as they did before. A few years from now you will not care for toys at all. Therefore, your parents will not bring you any toys. So you see, when you needed something, you got it; and when you do not need it, you won't get it. But I wish you to feel the need of light all your life so that God will always be most pleased with you and most proud of you.

*Question:* Why is it that I feel a difference between everyone else and my closest friend, God?

*Sri Chinmoy:* The difference that you notice between your closest friend, God, and your other friends is very simple. God thinks that you are as good as He is, as divine as He is and as perfect as He is. Your other friends think you may be good, divine and perfect; but they feel that they are better, more divine and more perfect than you are. All your human friends outwardly think and inwardly feel that you are not on their level. But you like them and they like you; you love them and they love you. That is why they are your friends and you are their friends. But in God's case, He loves you not only because you are His eternal friend, but because you and He are one.

*Question:* How can I be a good girl?

*Sri Chinmoy:* Every morning ask God to give you the strength and obedience you need to listen to your parents. You will pray to God to bless both you and your parents. You will ask God to be with you and around you twenty-four hours a day.

When you speak to God in your prayer, always think of God as being of your own age and standard. If you are four years old, then feel that He is four years old. If you feel that He is neither inferior nor superior to you, He can then tell you how you can be good.

*Question:* Who does God love the most?

*Sri Chinmoy:* God loves the child who loves Him most. Who loves Him most? He who has boundless love for God, boundless devotion for God and boundless surrender to God. What is love? What is devotion? What is surrender? Love is your cry for God. Devotion is your smile when you see God. Surrender is dancing with joy when God is in your presence.

*Question*: If someone does something bad and undivine, does God punish them or do they bring things on themselves?

*Sri Chinmoy*: If someone does bad, undivine things, God does not punish him the way we would. His punishment comes from some other place. Punishment comes from those whom we have deceived or from those to whom we do undivine things. It can also come from the world or place where certain forces exist. But God does not punish us when we do something wrong. On the contrary, when we do something wrong, He brings us a friend, light, and tells us, "If you mix with this friend and play with him all the time, then you will not do anything wrong. This friend will always tell you to do the right thing. But we do not like that friend; we ask him to go away. Again and again we do things wrong. Then forces around us and forces inside the person whom we have hurt try to punish us.

When we do something wrong, we find that we are inside a dark room. God comes into that room with a lantern. He says, "My child, take this lantern. If you keep it, you won't make the same mistake again." But we don't like this; we want to stay all by ourselves. So we take that lantern and throw it away. Our individuality is darkness, but we like it because it is ours. God brings us a friend to play with, which is light. If we stay with our friend light, then we will never make any mistakes. And since we won't make any mistakes, nobody will be able to punish us.

*Question:* Guru, if the Supreme is in everything, then He must also be in the mind. So why is the mind bad?

*Sri Chinmoy:* There are two minds. One mind is extremely nice, extremely divine, extremely pure. The other mind, which is in the physical, is not so divine and pure. When we say that the mind is not as good as the heart, we are speaking about the mind that is inside the body.

I am trying to simplify the matter. Otherwise it will become a philosophy. God is in everything. God is inside a tiger, but will you stand in front of a tiger? No! The tiger will just eat you up. God is inside everything, but in some things He is manifested to a greater degree.

You are a human being and I am also a human being. You eat rice, you eat bread, you eat pizza; I also eat these things. But in terms of inner realisation, there is a little difference between you and me; that is why you have come to me.

So the Supreme is in the mind also, but in the heart He is more accommodating, He is broader, He is kinder, He is more compassionate.

The heart and the soul love God much more than the mind. That is why we say that the heart and the soul are better. It is a comparison. The mind is not totally bad. If we don't have the mind, we won't be able to think and we will be like a fool. But there are quite a few things which are better than the mind. Better than the mind is the heart, and better than the heart is the soul. The heart is all oneness. If you remain inside the heart, you will not feel jealousy. You will have no suffering, no anxiety, no doubt, no jealousy. You are a sincere girl, so try always to have the heart that tells you, "We are all one, we are all one." Remain in the heart, pray in the heart, meditate in the heart.

Right now the mind is the boss. As long as your mind is the boss, it will make you feel miserable. But when you realise God, you will see that the mind is under your command. When you become the boss of the mind, at that time you are free.

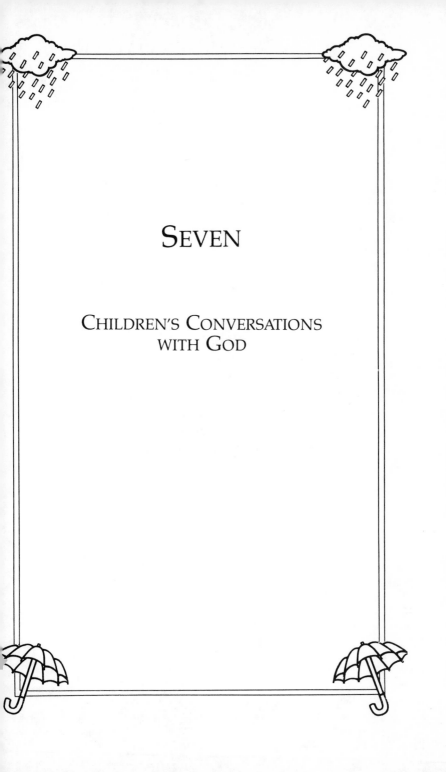

# SEVEN

## CHILDREN'S CONVERSATIONS WITH GOD

## INWARDLY YOU CAN TALK TO GOD

Inwardly you can talk to God
As long as you want to.
Therefore, talk, talk, talk!
Give Him all your sadness and frustration
    As well as your love and joy.
He will keep them all for you
    Inside His divine Heart-Safe.

# 7

"GOD, You have asked me to give away my toys to others. Not only my toys, but also many things I give away to people. And they take things from me gladly. But they do not say even one 'Thank you' to me."

"My child, I am so sorry to hear that. Don't worry, I shall scold them. But I thank you twice every day."

"God, when? Please tell me when You thank me."

"I thank you in silence through your father, when you give him a most beautiful smile before you go to bed at night. I thank you in silence through your mother, when you give her a most beautiful smile before you leave your bed early in the morning."

"God, I am a bit puzzled. My grandmother says that You are inside my heart. My mother says that You are inside my eyes. My father says that You are around me. Who is right, God?"

"All of them are right."

"Impossible, God! How can everybody be right? Please tell me frankly, who is right?"

"I tell you frankly, My child, your grandmother is right, your mother is right, your father is right."

"How?"

"I live inside your heart. That is why you are so soulful. I live inside your eyes. That is why you look spiritually beautiful. I live around you. That is why you are always so careful."

"God, You deserve my thanks."

"I don't deserve your thanks. It is your grandmother, your mother and your father who deserve your thanks. Go and thank them."

"I will. God, before I leave You, I wish to tell You one thing. Since You have always been very kind to me, You deserve my special thanks. My grandmother, mother and father will get ordinary thanks from me."

God smiles and cries with joy.

"God, my mother has told me not to make any complaints against anybody. But I am sorry, I have to. You know, God, my mother scolds me very often and my sister strikes me almost every day. I am sure they are not doing the right thing. What do You say, God?"

"Tell your sister and mother to speak to Me before they strike or scold you."

"Yes, yes, I shall do that. That means my sister will never be able to strike me. Neither will my mother be able to scold me."

"My child, it is not exactly so. Let Me tell you My secrets. When they ask Me for My permission to strike or scold you, I shall see first whether you deserve it or not. If you don't deserve it, I shall scold them badly. But if you deserve their scoldings and strikings, I shall give you enough strength and cheerfulness to eat the fruits of your wrong actions. I want you to be nice, good, perfect and divine."

"God, I shall be. Thanks and thanks, God."

"God, I have a real problem. My mother tells me that I must spend more time praying to You. My father tells me that the time that I spend in praying to You is more than enough. God, who is right, my mother or my father? Or are both of them wrong?"

"The more you pray, the more you please Me. So your father is wrong. Again, when you pray, if your heart is not in your prayer, then you are simply wasting time. So your mother is wrong if she insists on your praying when you have no sincere feeling in your prayer. Let Me give you a new prayer. This prayer will give you everything you want:

"'God, I pray to You to make me Your sweetest and dearest child. I pray to You to make me as kind as You are. I pray to You to make me listen to You every day. I pray to You to make me think of You always. I pray to You to give me the capacity to please You every day, every hour, every minute and every second.'"

"God, it is a terrific prayer. Can I add a few words?"

"Certainly you can, by all means!"

"God, I wish to add this: 'I love You, God. I worship You, God. I adore You, God.'"

"Amen. Wonderful, wonderful!"

"God, a million thanks. For sure I shall say every day the prayer that You have given me."

"God, my mother constantly bothers me. She tells me that I have to pray to You every morning and evening. She also says that if I do that, I shall be able to see You every day. She has told me something else. She has told me that You are very kind. If it's true, will You please do me a favour? Can You tell me how I can see You every day without praying to You?"

"I shall let you see Me not once, but twice a day. But you have to pray to Me a little. Wait, I have a nice idea. I am telling you secretly that I am going to give you the easiest prayer. You must not tell it to anybody; this is all between you and Me, a top secret.

"Every morning, stand in front of the large mirror in the living room and keep your eyes half open. Look at your eyes in the mirror and smile and smile. You are sure to see Me in your eyes. First you will see Me in your right eye, and then in your left eye."

"Will it always be like that? Can I not see You first in my left eye and then in my right eye?"

"Yes, but to do that, you have to keep both eyes closed, repeat My name seven times and then open your eyes. You are bound to see Me in your left eye first."

"God, do You mind if I do it the other way around? I hope You won't mind if I keep my eyes half open and smile until I see You, but not stand in front of the mirror. I think that will be easier. Do You mind?"

"No, not at all. I must say that you are wiser than I! I wanted to show you the easiest way to see Me. I wanted you to stand in front of the mirror and keep your eyes half open. You don't want to take even that much trouble. You just want to keep your eyes half open and smile until you see Me! You have discovered a way which is even easier! You are really clever and great, and that is why I am fond and proud of you."

"Thanks a lot, God."

"God, what is Your real name?"

"My real name is the same as yours."

"I won't give You my name!"

"Then what name do you want Me to have?"

"I want You to have the name Water."

"Water! That is a fine name. From now on, if you can call Me by that name, I shall respond."

"God, I'll tell You a secret. My mother has taught me that the other name of water is Life."

"Now, My child, I'll tell you another secret. The other name of life is God."

"Can I tell my mother Your secret?"

"Certainly you can."

"God, I really thank You for telling me a top secret."

"God, my grandfather always tells me that I must never tell a lie. But you know God, he has told me many lies."

"What are the lies that he has told you?"

"Number one lie: he told me that You are much older than he is. Number two lie: he told me that You don't need eyes to see like us. Number three lie: he told me that You don't need ears to hear like us. Number four lie: he told me that You don't need a mouth to talk.

"You are right in front of me. I see that You have two eyes, two ears and a mouth like me, and also I see that You are very young and beautiful. You are not even as old as my father. How can my grandfather tell me that You are older than he is?"

"My child, you are right. Your grandfather is also right. His knowledge of Me is from the books. Your knowledge of Me is from seeing Me face to face. Your grandfather takes Me as an idea. You see Me as a loving Friend and a living Truth."

"God, I wish to tell You something. Two thousand five hundred years ago there lived on earth a very, very great spiritual Master. His name was Buddha. I do think that You have heard his name. My father is a spiritual man. He follows the Buddha's path."

"Please tell Me, which path does your mother follow?"

"God, my mother follows many paths. She follows Buddha's path, Krishna's path, Ramakrishna's path, Ramana Maharshi's path and, at times, she follows Sri Chinmoy's path. By the way, God, these are all good and great spiritual Masters. They have many, many disciples and followers. God, I am now in a serious difficulty. I do not know which path I should follow. If I follow my father's path, the path of Zen, my father will be very pleased; and if I follow my mother's path, that is to say, many paths all at once, I shall please my mother."

"I wish you to follow My Path."

"What is Your Path, God?"

"Every day pray and meditate; I shall soon let you know what My Path is."

"God, I thank You from the bottom of my heart."

"God, do You have a minute? I have to ask You something. My mother says that I have to love You every single day. Is she right?"

"Yes, your mother is right."

"How can I love You when I don't know You very well?"

"Let Me tell you what to do. It is true that you don't know Me well, but you know your mother pretty well. From today on, try to love your mother more. The amount of love that she needs from you she will keep for herself and the rest she will give to Me. We shall share your love. Okay?"

"Thank You, God."

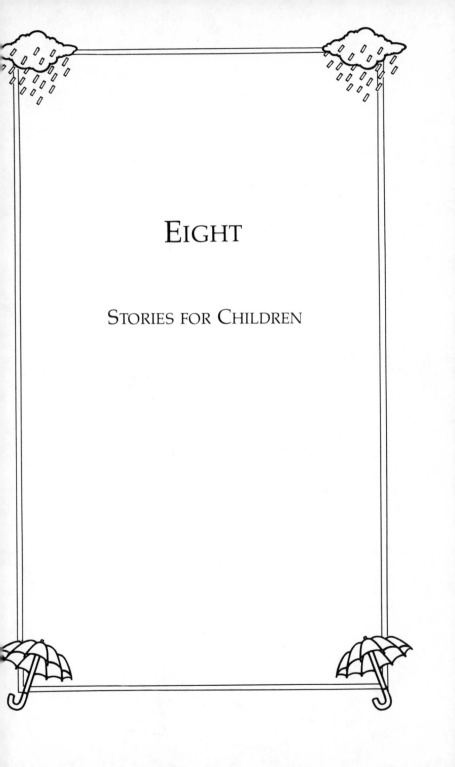

# EIGHT

## STORIES FOR CHILDREN

# 8

## GOPAL'S BROTHER

THIS is a very beautiful story. It is a story about Krishna. Krishna has another name, Rakhal Raja. 'Raja' means king, and 'rakhal' means cowherd—one who takes the cows to the pastures to graze. Krishna was a king and he was also a cowherd, so he was called Rakhal Raja, King of the Cowherds.

Once there lived an elderly man who was kind, generous and pious. He used to pray to God every day. When he became very old and was about to die, he said to his wife, "I am dying. I will leave you here on earth, but don't worry. God will take care of you."

His wife replied, "You are going to Heaven, but don't worry. God will take care of you there."

This elderly couple had only one child, a little boy named Gopal. He was seven years old when his father died. This little family had always lived in the forest. They were very poor and had only one cow. After Gopal's father died, his mother used to sell the milk from the cow to get some money. With this money she fed Gopal and herself. Although she was very, very poor, she was a great devotee of Lord Krishna. She prayed to Lord Krishna twenty-four hours a day. She never forgot him for a moment. Her entire life was a prayer.

Because Gopal was seven years old, he had to begin going to school. The school was quite far from his home, so he had to go through the thick of the forest to get there. There were wild animals all around, and naturally he was afraid. He went to school in the morning with great fear and difficulty and when he came back in the evening, it was worse. At that time there was little light and he was even more afraid. He came home trembling and practically weeping with fear.

One day he said to his mother, "I am not going to school anymore. I am afraid. You have to send someone with me or I will not go anymore."

His mother replied, "My child, tomorrow your elder brother will be with you. I have another son. He stays in the thick of the forest and you will see him with the cows. When you call him, he will come and play with you. He will take you to the school and he will bring you home again."

Gopal was so happy. He asked his mother, "What is the name of my brother whom I have not seen?"

"Your brother's name is Rakhal Raja," said his mother.

The following day when Gopal entered the thick of the forest on his way to school, he called out, "Rakhal Raja, Rakhal Raja, where are you?" Rakhal Raja immediately came. He

looked like a real king, with a crown and a peacock feather.

So Rakhal Raja met Gopal and they went
together to the school. When they came near
the school building, Rakhal Raja said to Gopal,
"Now you go on. I will come to take you home
when school is over." In this way, every day
Rakhal Raja took Gopal to school in the
morning and brought him back home safely in
the evening. Gopal was delighted with his new
brother.

One day his mother asked him, "Gopal, does
Rakhal Raja come?"

"Yes, he comes," said Gopal.

"I told you he would come. He is your elder
brother," said his mother.

Both Rakhal Raja and Gopal were very
happy together. They played all sorts of games
in the forest. Rakhal used to bring nice sweets
and all kinds of good things for his little
brother, so Gopal was always happy and
pleased. When he came home late his mother
was not worried because his elder brother
Rakhal Raja was taking care of him.

After a few months, Gopal's schoolteacher
lost his mother. In India, when somebody dies,
a festival is held at the end of the month.
Everybody comes and has a feast. You eat as
much as you can, and if you don't want to eat,
they force you. So a month after the schoolteacher's mother died, there was a feast for the
schoolchildren. Naturally, all the students were
bringing presents to the teacher. Gopal knew
that everybody was going to bring a present for
the schoolteacher, but poor Gopal didn't have
any money. He asked his mother sadly, "What
can I do? I wish to take something to my

teacher, but we are so poor. What can I do?"

"Ask your Rakhal Raja," said Gopal's mother. "He will give you something to give to your teacher."

In the morning while Rakhal Raja was taking Gopal to school, Gopal said to him, "Rakhal Raja, today everyone will give a gift to the teacher, but I am too poor. Can you give me something?"

Rakhal Raja said, "I am also very poor, but I will give you something." Gopal was happy to have anything that he could give his teacher.

Rakhal Raja, who was really a god, immediately placed before Gopal a small pot of sour milk, or curd. It is something like what you call yoghurt. "Take this," he said. "Your teacher knows that you are very poor. He will not mind."

Gopal was happy that at least he had something to give to his teacher. But, poor boy, when he came to school, he saw that his fellow students had all brought expensive and beautiful things. So he was very sad and embarrassed, and he stood at the door like a thief. He did not want anybody to see him because he had brought only a little sour milk in a small pot. But the teacher was extremely kind. He took the little pot from Gopal and poured the sour milk into a large pot. He thought that his servants would soon bring sour milk for the festival and that it could be added to the small potful that Gopal had brought.

But what happened? When the teacher emptied the sour milk from the little pot into the big pot, the sour milk suddenly increased in quantity and filled the big pot to the brim! The teacher was astonished that this tiny little amount of sour milk had become so vast.

During the festival the people who ate the sour milk from Gopal kept exclaiming how good it was. "We have never tasted anything like this!" they said. "It is so fragrant and delightful! The flavour is delicious! It is simply excellent!"

The teacher said, "Gopal brought it for me. It was Gopal's gift." Then he asked Gopal, "Where did you get the pot of sour milk that you gave me?"

Gopal replied, "My Rakhal Raja gave it to me."

"Who is your Rakhal Raja?" asked the teacher.

"Oh, Rakhal Raja is my brother. He is my most intimate friend. He always comes with me to school and takes me back home," said Gopal.

The teacher knew that Gopal had no brother. He had only one relative and that was his mother. So he asked, "Can you show me your Rakhal Raja?"

"Yes," replied Gopal. "He is most beautiful. He has a crown, with a peacock feather in it. He is so beautiful!" Gopal promised the teacher that he would take him to Rakhal Raja. "Yes, you come with me, Sir," he said. "I will take you to my Rakhal Raja."

In the evening, when the festival was over and everybody had eaten and gone home, Gopal took his teacher along with him to the forest. At the usual place where he used to meet his older brother, he cried out, "Rakhal Raja, Rakhal Raja, Rakhal Raja!" But Rakhal Raja did not come to him.

He called again, "Rakhal Raja, why are you
so naughty? Every day you come here even if I
don't call you. Today I am crying for you and
you are not coming. Why are you so unkind to
me? Why are you so cruel? My teacher will not
believe me. He will think that I am a liar.
Please come, Rakhal Raja, please come." He
cried and begged, but Rakhal Raja did not
appear.

The teacher said, "You are a liar. Somebody
else has given this to you."

Gopal shook his head and said, "No, no, my
Rakhal Raja has given it to me. I don't know
why he is angry with me today. I don't know
why he is not coming to me." And again he
started calling, "Rakhal Raja, please, please,
come!" But Rakhal Raja would not come.

Then Gopal and the teacher heard a voice
from the forest saying, "Gopal, today I won't
come. I come to you because of your mother.
Your mother prays to me every day. She prays
to me all the time. I am extremely pleased with
your mother, and that is why I come to help
you and play with you. But your teacher has
never prayed to me. Why should I show my
face to him? Your teacher does not deserve me.
I am only for those who pray to me, for those
who need me. Your teacher has never prayed to
me, so I will not come."

The teacher understood, and he was
extremely pleased that Gopal's mother was so
spiritual. He could not see Lord Krishna
himself, but he knew that there was somebody
who could see him because she prayed to him
every day, and that person was Gopal's
mother.

You too can pray in the morning and in the evening. If you pray in the morning and in the evening, then God will be pleased. Pray for five minutes in the morning and in the evening. Your mother or your father will teach you how. When you do it, you will see that you will get your own Rakhal Raja to help you whenever you are in difficulty or danger.

## PRAY FOR PROTECTION

One day a young boy of twelve or thirteen was attacked by fifteen mischievous, naughty boys and girls while he was walking home from school. The poor boy was all alone and quite helpless. How could he defend himself against so many naughty boys and girls? He thought of what his mother had often told him: "Whenever you are in difficulty or danger, pray to God." He prayed to God for a second or two, but there was no help from God, and he was cruelly beaten.

He went home crying and crying. His mother consoled him and he said to her, "You told me that if I prayed to God, God would protect me. But God didn't protect me. Look, I am black and blue, and my body is bleeding in so many places!"

His mother said, "My son, I told you to pray to God every day, but you do not. You do not pray every day early in the morning and in the evening. You pray to God perhaps once a week, and sometimes you don't even pray that often. Sometimes you meditate one day and then for ten or fifteen days you don't meditate.

"You have to pray to God every day for at least ten minutes early in the morning.

Meditation and prayer are like muscles. If you take exercise one day, and then for ten days you don't take exercise, then you cannot become strong. Only if you take exercise every day will you become strong. In the same way, if you pray to God every day, your inner muscles will become stronger and God will protect you. God is bound to protect you if you pray to Him every day early in the morning and in the evening."

From that day on, the young boy started praying to God. He listened to what his mother had said and he prayed to God every day. Early in the morning he prayed for ten minutes and in the evening also he prayed for five minutes. After doing this for six months he said to his mother, "Yes, prayer works. Nobody bothers me now. I come home every day, but nobody ever bothers me."

His mother said, "Even if somebody does bother you, I tell you, you will be protected because you have been praying regularly every day, and God is pleased with you. God will protect you."

Now, on that very day something happened. When the boy was going home from school, a very tall, big, stout man grabbed him roughly and wanted to strike him. The boy immediately thought, "O God, my mother told me that if I pray to You every day You will protect me," and he started repeating the Lord's Name very loudly: "God, God, God, God, save me, save me!"

The fellow who had caught him was a very big, strong man, and he laughed at the boy, saying, "What do you think you are doing by saying 'God, God, God'? Do you think that you can get rid of me in that way? No, you can't!"

All of a sudden a voice from inside the boy said to him, "Tell this man that even a ghost leaves when we repeat God's Name." The boy quickly said what the inner voice had told him, and the man immediately let go of him and ran away.

The previous night this man had had a dream in which he saw a ghost, and he had been badly frightened. Everyone is afraid of ghosts, even grown-ups. Hearing the word 'ghost' reminded the man of the ghost that he had seen the night before. When the boy said, "Even a ghost leaves when you repeat God's Name," God made the hoodlum actually see this young boy as the ghost of his dream. God showed him the ghost in the face of the little boy, so he ran away.

When the man left him, the boy ran home to tell the story to his mother. His mother said, "It is just as I told you. If you pray to God every day, God will save you. He will protect you."

So you see, if you pray daily, God will protect you. This little boy never thought of a ghost, but God told him what to say. If you pray, God will play divine tricks and He will help you when you are in danger. God will give you some message from within or He will give the other person some message. If someone attacks you, immediately you will say something which you do not understand. When you say it, the other fellow will be scared to death and he will leave you. Pray to God every day and when you are in difficulty God will tell you what to do.

# A CHILD'S GOD

*By Mridu Bhashini Devi*
*(Translated from the original Bengali*
*by Sri Chinmoy)*

Gulu had completed his fourth year and stepped into his fifth. He had been introduced to the alphabet. Gulu's father said, "Well, Gulu, I shall now put you in the primary school of the schoolmaster Aghore."

Gulu's joy knew no bounds. Now he would go to school with a satchel under his arm.

Gulu was very intelligent, and he was very fond of stories. He often teased his grandmother to tell him stories. She told him the story of Prahlad and he listened to her words with wonder and implicit faith. The whole story filled his mind. Gulu said, "How cruel is the father of Prahlad, Grandmother! What tortures he has inflicted on Prahlad! But nobody can slay him who has God for his helper."

One day it occurred to Gulu to find God. "As God is worshipped with flowers, He must be hiding in the roses in the garden," Gulu reflected. "Once I am able to discover God, I will so befriend Him that He will not be able to desert me anymore."

Gulu spent the day in the garden, shaking the plants in his search for God. But he met Him nowhere. At last he returned home disappointed.

Gulu asked his mother, "I search for God so much. Why do I not find Him, Mother?"

"Gulu, God is fond of playing. So He plays hide-and-seek with us. He is an expert player. He hides Himself in such a way that even the great saints and sages fail to find Him."

"Who then can discover Him, Mother?"

"Nobody can find Him unless He reveals Himself. Still He stays with each and every one and protects all as He did Prahlad. He hides Himself in your heart, too."

"In the core of my heart! Believe me, Mother, when I search for Him in the garden it seems someone responds from within my heart."

"It is this indweller who is God. Adore Him. Learn to love Him as you love me. He is there not only in your heart but in all hearts. Learn to love all, then He will surely reveal Himself to you."

Gulu's mind was set at rest by the words of his mother. He cherished the hope that someday God would come to him.

One day, Gulu and his mother visited his maternal uncle's house. The three of them returned home on the eve of the Pujas. The train was packed with passengers and there was not enough room. Gulu was not concerned about that. He hung out of the window to gaze at the scenery. His uncle said, "Don't bend forward like that. You may fall out, Gulu."

"How can I fall? I am holding onto the door."

Suddenly the door somehow opened out. Unable to check himself, Gulu fell outside. People inside the compartment raised cries of horror and lamentation. Gulu's mother, under the spell of despair, was about to jump from the train, but someone held her back.

It was nighttime. Nothing was visible in the dark. The train was running at top speed. Owing to the excitement, no one thought of pulling the chain to stop the train. Alerted by the confused noise, the passengers in the next compartment pulled the chain. The motion of the train was immediately arrested.

The train went backward. Nobody hoped to see Gulu alive. After some distance had been covered a figure became visible on a bridge. Gulu's mother cried out, "Look, my Gulu is there!"

The train stopped. Gulu's mother rushed up to him and took him in her arms. "Did you get hurt, Gulu?" she cried.

"How can I be hurt, Mother? The moment I fell down, my uncle jumped and took me in his arms."

In a surprised voice the mother said, "Your uncle did not come down. He was there inside."

"Don't tell a lie, Mother! All this time my uncle held me on his lap. As you all drew near he put me down and went that way. You can look for him."

A thrill passed through the whole body of Gulu's mother. She said, "Gulu, God saved you in the form of your uncle." At the words of his mother, Gulu was beside himself with wonder.

So God is bound to come to you when you are in real difficulty if you pray to Him every day. If you pray to God every day, then you will see God's most beautiful Form. When you see God face to face, you will be surprised because He is infinitely more beautiful than you can imagine.

To pray to God, you don't have to ask your parents for anything. In order to buy shirts or shoes or anything else, you need money. But in order to see God, you don't need money; you only need prayer. Prayer is so easy. It is like drinking water. Just pray and you will get Him. When you get Him, you will get everything you need.

## ABOUT SRI CHINMOY

Sri Chinmoy is a fully realised spiritual Master dedicated to inspiring and serving those seeking a deeper meaning in life. Through his teaching of meditation, lectures and writings, and through his own life of dedicated service to humanity, he tries to show others how to find inner peace and fulfilment.

Born in Bengal in 1931, Sri Chinmoy entered an ashram (spiritual community) at the age of 12. His life of intense spiritual practice included meditating for up to 14 hours a day, together with writing poetry, essays and devotional songs, doing selfless service and practising athletics. While still in his early teens, he had many profound inner experiences and attained spiritual realisation. He remained in the ashram for 20 years, deepening and expanding his realisation, and in 1964 came to New York City to share his inner wealth with sincere seekers.

Today, Sri Chinmoy serves as a spiritual guide to disciples in some 80 centres around the world. He teaches the "Path of the Heart," which he feels is the simplest way to make rapid spiritual progress. By meditating on the spiritual heart, he teaches, the seeker can discover his own inner treasures of peace, joy, light and love. The role of a spiritual Master, according to Sri Chinmoy, is to help the seeker live so that these inner riches can illumine his life. Sri Chinmoy lovingly instructs his disciples in the inner life and elevates their consciousness not only beyond their expectation, but even beyond their imagination. In return he asks his students to meditate regularly and to try to nurture the inner qualities he brings to the fore in them.

Sri Chinmoy teaches that love is the most direct way for a seeker to approach the Supreme. When a child feels love for his father, it does not matter how great the father is in the world's eye; through his love the child feels only his oneness with his father and his father's possessions. This same approach, applied to the Supreme, permits the seeker to feel that the Supreme and His own Eternity, Infinity and Immortality are the seeker's own. This philosophy of love, Sri Chinmoy feels, expresses the deepest bond between man and God, who are aspects of the same unified consciousness. In the life-game, man fulfils himself in the Supreme by realising that He is his own highest self. The Supreme reveals Himself through man, who serves as His instrument for world transformation and perfection.

Sri Chinmoy's path does not end with realisation. Once we realise the highest, it is still necessary to manifest this reality in the world around us. In Sri Chinmoy's words, "To

2

climb up the mango tree is great, but it is not enough. We have to climb down again to distribute the mangoes and make the world aware of their significance. Until we do this, our role is not complete and God will not be satisfied or fulfilled."

In the traditional Indian fashion, Sri Chinmoy does not charge a fee for his spiritual guidance, nor does he charge for his frequent lectures, concerts or public meditations. His only fee, he says, is the seeker's sincere inner cry. Sri Chinmoy takes a personal interest in each of his students, and when he accepts a disciple, he takes full responsibility for that seeker's inner progress. In New York, Sri Chinmoy meditates in person with his disciples several times each week and offers a regular Wednesday evening meditation session for the general public. Students living outside New York see Sri Chinmoy during worldwide gatherings that take place three times a year, during visits to New York, or during the Master's frequent trips to their cities. Most find that the inner bond between Master and disciple transcends physical separation.

As part of his selfless offering to humanity, Sri Chinmoy conducts peace meditations twice each week for ambassadors and staff at United Nations Headquarters in New York. He also conducts peace meditations for government officials at the United States Congress in Washington, D.C.

In addition, Sri Chinmoy leads an active life, demonstrating most vividly that spirituality is not an escape from the world, but a means of transforming it. He has written more than 700 books, which include plays, poems, stories,

3

essays, commentaries and answers to questions on spirituality. He has painted some 140,000 widely exhibited mystical paintings and composed more than 5,000 devotional songs.

Sri Chinmoy accepts students at all levels of development, from beginners to advanced seekers, and lovingly guides them inwardly and outwardly according to their individual needs. For further information please write to:

Aum Publications
86-24 Parsons Blvd.
Jamaica, N.Y. 11432

## BOOKS AND TAPES BY SRI CHINMOY

*Meditation: Man-Perfection in God-Satisfaction*, $6.95

If you do not have a Guru of your own, this complete, practical guide to meditation, which leads the student from the beginning stages to the most advanced practices, is the next best thing. Descriptions of simple yet powerful meditation techniques are amplified by answers to the questions most commonly asked by seekers. Sri Chinmoy explains how to find inner peace, the secrets of will power and concentration, the process of opening the spiritual heart and the meaning of various inner experiences and visions.

*Sri Chinmoy Plays the Flute* (Cassette), $8.95

While in a state of deep meditation, Sri Chinmoy plays his haunting music on the echo flute, transporting the listener to beautiful realms of inner peace and harmony. With its rich and soothing tones, the music seems to have as its source an endless wellspring whose currents evoke the mystery and power of the universe. An excellent aid to meditation.

*Inner and Outer Peace*, $5.95

In this book Sri Chinmoy speaks of the higher truths that energise the quest for world peace, giving contemporary expression to the interrelationship between inner and outer peace. Topics include: the struggle for world peace, the answer to world despair, the path to personal peace, overcoming the threat of nuclear destruction, and more. On the companion cassette tape, Sri Chinmoy weaves a beautiful tapestry of his poetry and aphorisms on inner and outer peace with his own uplifting music on the esraj, echo flute, harmonium and synthesizer ($8.95).

*The Master and the Disciple*, $3.95

What is a Guru? For those in search of spiritual enlightenment, the Guru is more than an "expert"; he is the way to their self-realisation. Sri Chinmoy says in this definitive book on the Guru-disciple relationship, "The most important thing a spiritual Master does for his spiritual children is to make them consciously aware of something vast and infinite within themselves, which is nothing other than God Himself." Finding the Guru who is meant for you, spiritual initiation, and how the Guru illumines his disciples are just a few of the topics covered in this informative book.

*Beyond Within: A Philosophy for the Inner Life*, *$10.95 (500 pages)*

When your yearning to know the purpose of life and the reality of God has you swimming against the tide, then the wisdom of one who has swum these waters is priceless. In this book, Sri Chinmoy leads the way, with sound advice on how to integrate your highest spiritual aspirations into your daily life. Covering most of the major areas of concern to the seeker, such as: the inner voice, discipline, realisation, the mind and the heart, liberation, the play of inner forces and much more.

*My Lord's Secrets Revealed, $5.00*
*($10.00 hardbound)*

In this series of "conversations" between God and one of his fondest children, Sri Chinmoy reveals the deepest philosophy in the simplest, most heartfelt terms. You'll want to read this book again and again. Beautifully designed and illustrated.

"*My Lord's Secrets Revealed* is a collection of short, personal conversations with God, which are truly in the *bhakti* spirit—full of devotion, humor, child-like innocence and sweetness."

*Saturday Review*

*Yoga and the Spiritual Life, $4.95*

Perhaps the most comprehensive introduction to the philosophical underpinnings of yoga and spirituality. In this book Sri Chinmoy presents a clear and moving explanation of the timeless relevance of India's age-old mystical tradition to everyday life. There is something for everyone, from the beginning seeker to the advanced aspirant.

*Astrology, the Supernatural and the Beyond, $3.95*

At last, a book that speaks with full spiritual authority on such controversial topics as astrology, the occult, psychic power, the supernatural and cosmic forces. Sri Chinmoy describes in clear and simple language the unseen forces that operate in and around us, and how to welcome the positive influences, while protecting ourselves from the negative ones. A must for anyone interested in astrology, occultism or any aspect of the inner life.

*Death and Reincarnation: Eternity's Voyage, $3.95*

This deeply moving, spellbinding book pulls aside the veil that has hidden the mysteries of death. Based on his mystical vision and meditative ability to travel through the world of death and beyond, Sri Chinmoy explains through examples the simple yet previously unfathomable secrets of death, the afterlife and reincarnation. This book has offered limitless consolation and hope to thousands faced with the passing of loved ones or fear of their own mortality.

*Kundalini: The Mother Power, $3.95*

Kundalini, the ancient yogic practice that opens the chakras and confers inner powers, is described in this fascinating collection of lectures delivered by Sri Chinmoy under the auspices of the New York University Department of Religion. Sri Chinmoy explains different techniques to awaken the powers of kundalini, describes how the pitfalls and dangers of this approach can be avoided and reveals the occult powers that come with the flowering of the chakras. With questions and answers.

*Eastern Light for the Western Mind, $3.95*

An illumined collection of lectures given by Sri Chinmoy at Oxford, Cambridge, Harvard, Yale and thirty-eight other universities in the United States and abroad. These compelling talks reveal the timeless wisdom of the East in a format tailored to the Western seeker. Delivered by Sri Chinmoy in high meditative states, they describe the secret of inner peace, intuition, consciousness, inner and outer freedom and other fascinating topics.

*Songs of the Soul, $5.00 ($10.00 hardbound)*

If you were aware of what your soul is telling you, your life's problems would end. You would know what to do all the time and have the courage to do it. To help you discover your own soul's truth, Sri Chinmoy has distilled the essence of his own inner experiences in this rare and illumining book. The deep wisdom offered here reveals the inmost mysteries of the soul and serves as an unwavering guide for all on the spiritual path. A cassette of passages from this book read by the author to the accompaniment of a choir, orchestra and jazz guitar is also available ($8.95).

*Eternity's Breath*, $5.00

A spiritual classic, continuously in print since 1972. This book of short essays and aphorisms contains some of Sri Chinmoy's most inspiring and spiritually uplifting writings. Some of the more than 50 topics covered include: the soul, matter and spirit, man and woman, ambition, death, spiritual discipline, courage, grace and compassion.

*The Outer Running and the Inner Running*, $6.95

Sri Chinmoy is unique among spiritual Masters in the way he has integrated sports with spiritual development in an all-encompassing philosophy of life. In this book, he shows the many parallels between spirituality—what he calls the inner running—and sports, or the outer running. He gives specific advice, from a spiritual point of view, to both inner and outer runners.                                    9

*The Summits of God-Life: Samadhi and Siddhi,*
$3.95

While still a youth in India, Sri Chinmoy had his first deep encounters with the Absolute, entering states of awareness in which his whole being merged with the Universal Consciousness. Gradually, through years of spiritual discipline, he achieved mastery over these realms. This book is his first-hand account of states of consciousness that only a handful of Masters through the ages have ever experienced.

If you wish to order any of the above books or tapes, please send a check or money order made payable to Aum Publications. Add a postage charge of $1.30 for the first item and $.30 for each additional item. Send to the following address:

Aum Publications
86-24 Parsons Blvd.
Jamaica, N.Y. 11432